Arthur W. H. Eaton

The Church of England in Nova Scotia

and the Tory clergy of the Revolution

Arthur W. H. Eaton

The Church of England in Nova Scotia
and the Tory clergy of the Revolution

ISBN/EAN: 9783337228255

Printed in Europe, USA, Canada, Australia, Japan

Cover: Foto ©Lupo / pixelio.de

More available books at www.hansebooks.com

THE
CHURCH OF ENGLAND

IN NOVA SCOTIA

AND THE

TORY CLERGY OF THE REVOLUTION

BY

ARTHUR WENTWORTH EATON, B.A.

PRESBYTER OF THE DIOCESE OF NEW YORK

SECOND EDITION.

NEW YORK
THOMAS WHITTAKER
1892.

TO THE

People of St. James' Church

KENTVILLE

AMONG WHOM I WORSHIPPED IN BOYHOOD

WITH LOVING MEMORIES

I DEDICATE THIS BOOK

PREFACE.

THE history of Nova Scotia has a unique and varied interest, which likewise extends to the Church of England in this Province. On the Church in Nova Scotia, practically nothing has been written; a valuable sketch by the late Dr. Thomas B. Akins, long out of print, and a brief account of the early history of the Church in New Brunswick, by Mr. George Herbert Lee, are the only published writings directly on the subject. In the United States there should be much interest in the Diocese of Nova Scotia, for that Diocese owes its existence to the Tories of the Revolution, who went in thousands from New York and Massachusetts to the "Acadian Province by the Sea," and its first bishop was, at the outbreak of the war, the honored rector of the leading Church in the older Colonies.

The attention I have given to biography, in this volume, has seemed to me necessary from the fact that the Church in Nova Scotia, which has been quite out of the range of great movements of thought, and great events, has had, notwithstanding, among its clergy and laity, a large number of distinguished men. Many of its early clergy were highly educated and able men, who at the Revolution left comfortable parishes in the older Colonies for raw missions in the Nova Scotia and New Brunswick wilds, and long and manfully did the Church's work on these new shores. Many of its laymen were also persons of note in the Colonies from which they came, and resuming public life in Nova Scotia, in their new field showed the same energy of character and marked ability they had shown before. I was born too late to do more than catch faint echoes of Tory times, but in boyhood I worshipped in one of the old Parish Churches in the Acadian Land, which had about it all the atmosphere of Colonial Days —an atmosphere that lasted long in Nova Scotia—and my vivid recollections of the dignified worship, and my love for the worshippers, has made the writing of this book a very pleasant task. It was my first intention to write brief sketches of the various parishes in the Diocese, but from lack of response to my circulars, and for other reasons, I soon changed my plan, and so have been obliged to omit many local details that would necessarily have been given in a more statistical account of the Church in Nova Scotia. I have, however, gathered many documents and pamphlets that would be useful for such a work, and shall deposit them, together with the reports of the S. P. G., which I have had copied in New York and in London, in the Provincial Library at Halifax.

In the biographical work in this volume my indebtedness to Sabine's " History of the Loyalists " will be readily seen ; but I have likewise been helped in the preparation of biographies by Sprague's " Annals of the American Pulpit," Bolton's " History of Westchester County," Beardsley's " History of the Church in Connecticut," the records of Harvard, Yale, and Columbia colleges, where the greater number of the Tory clergy and many of the leading Loyalist laymen were educated, and by many pamphlets and small publications in Nova Scotia and New Brunswick, which are hardly to be found outside these provinces. The strictly historical work in this book has been made easier by two Nova Scotians, to whom every year gives me a deeper sense of indebtedness; the late Mr. Beamish Murdock, whose three volume documentary history of Nova Scotia contains untold historical treasures; and the late Dr. Thomas Beamish Akins, the painstaking Record Commissioner of the Province, largely through whom the great wealth of manuscripts in the Provincial Library at Halifax has been made available for the purposes of historical research. For many of the details of such a work as this, the careful Reports of the Society for the Propagation of the Gospel are, necessarily, the chief source of authority.

"AN infant Church is rising under the favour and protection of Government in Nova Scotia; and it is of a singular description, consisting of Honourable Exiles, under the pastoral care of Fellow-Sufferers."

THE BISHOP OF OXFORD, *in a sermon preached before the S. P. G. February* 20, 1784.

CONTENTS.

CHAP.		PAGE
I.	THE ANNAPOLIS GARRISON,	1
II.	HALIFAX AND THE VENERABLE SOCIETY,	25
III.	THE CHURCH ESTABLISHED,	38
IV.	HISTORIC ST. PAUL'S,	53
V.	FOUR EARLY MISSIONS,	67
VI.	THE COMING OF THE LOYALISTS,	95
VII.	THE FIRST COLONIAL BISHOP,	109
VIII.	THE CHURCH AT SHELBURNE,	135
IX.	THE NEW TORY PROVINCE,	145
X.	EXILED CLERGY OF THE REVOLUTION,	155
XI.	KING'S COLLEGE,	191
XII.	THE CHURCH'S GROWTH,	215
XIII.	LATER BISHOPS,	227
XIV.	DISTINGUISHED LAYMEN,	245
XV.	OTHER RELIGIOUS BODIES,	269
XVI.	ROYAL GOVERNORS OF NOVA SCOTIA,	289

IMPORTANT DATES.

1713. The Treaty of Utrecht, by which Acadia was finally ceded to the British Crown.

1749. The Founding of Halifax by Colonel, afterward Lord, Edward Cornwallis.

1758. The Fall of Louisburg which led to the final possession by England of the Island of Cape Breton (Isle Royale), and the Island of St. John (Prince Edward Island).

1763. Annexation of the Islands of Cape Breton and St. John to the Government of Nova Scotia.

1784. New Brunswick set off from Nova Scotia, and Colonel Thomas Carleton made its Governor.

1784. November 14th, Bishop Seabury consecrated at Aberdeen.

1787. February 4th, Bishops White and Prevoost consecrated at Lambeth.

1787. August 12th, Bishop Charles Inglis consecrated at Lambeth, his jurisdiction to extend over the Provinces of Nova Scotia (including Cape Breton), New Brunswick, Prince Edward Island, Upper and Lower Canada, and Newfoundland, besides the Bermuda Islands.

1793. The Diocese of Quebec founded, comprising the whole of Canada. This Diocese was divided, in 1850, into two Dioceses, Quebec and Montreal.

1816. Bishop Stanser consecrated at Lambeth.

1825. March 27th, Bishop John Inglis consecrated at Lambeth.

1839. The Diocese of Newfoundland founded (including Labrador and Bermuda).

1839. The Diocese of Toronto founded, comprising the whole of Upper Canada. In this territory there are now five Dioceses— Toronto, Huron, Ontario, Niagara, and Algoma.

1845. The Diocese of Fredericton founded.

1851. March 25th, Bishop Binney consecrated at Lambeth.

1888. April 25th, Bishop Courtney consecrated at Halifax.

The Church in Nova Scotia.

CHAPTER I.

THE ANNAPOLIS GARRISON.

NOVA SCOTIA has the dignity of being the oldest Colonial diocese of the Church of England, her first bishop having been the first bishop consecrated for England's loyal children in any of the growing colonies of her empire in the East or the West. Except Connecticut, New York, and Pennsylvania, she is the eldest, indeed, of that great sisterhood of Anglican dioceses, that from four continents now claim the Church in England as their mother. On this account, if on no other, the history of the diocese of Nova Scotia should command the interest of Anglican Churchmen everywhere. But there are facts other than ecclesiastical about this sea-girt province that lend interest to its church history. Nova Scotia is the ancient Acadia, the camping ground of two great nations that for more than a century fiercely contended for supremacy in these western wilds. To Acadia France sent some of her most adventurous spirits, some of her bravest explorers, some of the gayest and courtliest of her nobles. In her welfare were interested the proudest of France's sovereigns, the greatest of her statesmen, the most influential of her priests, the most brilliant women of her Tuileries and Versailles. About the old Acadian forts cluster many of those romantic traditions of love and sorrow that France always left where she planted her lilies. In the conquest and settlement of Acadia, England exhibited some of her most marked traits—indomitable energy, undaunted courage, military ardor, and a genius for successful colonization. To her Acadian possessions many of her sturdy sons turned their steps for trade and agriculture, and in the conquered forts, first and last, dwelt many who bore the greatest English names. To the interest that such traditions give, one must add the charm of quiet scenery—rich alluvial dyke lands, well-tilled upland farms, and orchards in the midst of which nestle homes that remind travellers of the homes in the

Greek islands, as they appear to those who sail by; slight mountain ridges that end in bold, picturesque headlands; gracefully indented coasts, blue bays and harbors with green slopes to their edges, long lilied lake chains where, for days, one may row unhindered from point to point; luxuriant pine and maple woods, with autumn colors more brilliant than elsewhere, and wild flowers with crisper, clearer tints.

Acadia was originally a region of undetermined extent, in a general way embracing the maritime provinces—Nova Scotia, New Brunswick, and Prince Edward Island, part of the province of Lower Canada, or Quebec, and part of Maine. In the treaty of Utrecht its boundaries are given as, south, the Atlantic Ocean, west, a line drawn due north from the mouth of the Penobscot, north, the St. Lawrence river, east, the Gulf of St. Lawrence and the Strait of Canso. Of all this tract of country De Monts was named, in 1603, lieutenant-general, his powers likewise extending to all the inhabitable shores of America north of the latitude of Philadelphia. His first settlement, which was soon abandoned, was on St. Croix island, in the St. Croix River, his second, which was permanent, was Port Royal, on the Annapolis basin. With De Monts, in this first settlement were associated Champlain, Pontgravé, and Jean de Poutrincourt. In 1613, Captain Samuel Argall, an Englishman, engaged in settling Virginia, came north and wantonly destroyed the little French colony at Mt. Desert, established by the Countess de Guercheville for converting the Indians, and the next year came farther on and tried to destroy Port Royal. In 1621, England having gained nominal possession of Acadia, Sir William Alexander, a Scotchman, obtained from James I. a charter of "New Scotland," comprising Nova Scotia and New Brunswick, and made several attempts to colonize his domain. To put new life into the enterprise he parcelled out the territory into baronetcies, and established the order of Baronets of Nova Scotia. In 1632, by the treaty of St. Germain's, Britain surrendered the territory to France, Alexander's rights having been previously bought by Claude and his son, Charles de la Tour. Shortly after the peace, Chevalier Razilly was made by Louis XIII. governor of the whole of Acadia, appointing as his lieutenants Charles de la Tour, east of the St. Croix, and Charles de Menon, Sieur d'Aulnay-Charnisé, west. The former established himself on the river St. John, the latter at Castine, on the eastern shore of Penobscot Bay, and one of the most romantic chapters in Acadian history is the long story of their quarrels, of the brave defense of her husband's fort by Madame de la Tour, of her death soon after from grief and humiliation, then of Charnisé's death, and two or three years later of his widow's marriage to her husband's old rival, de la Tour. In 1654, under Cromwell, Acadia was subjugated by two Puritans, Major Robert Sedgwick of Charlestown, Massachusetts, and Captain John Leverett of Boston, and in 1656 Sir Thomas Temple, one of Cromwell's supporters, was made its governor. In 1668, by the treaty of Breda, it was again ceded to France with undefined limits, and again in 1690, Port Royal was conquered by Sir William Phips, who became soon after the first royal governor of Massachusetts. Once more, in 1697, by the treaty of Ryswick, Acadia was handed back to France, to be restored finally to England in 1713.

Apart from the few French or English who from time to time settled in Acadia, the country was originally inhabited solely by various tribes of the Algonquin family of Indians, for the most part naturally quiet, harmless people, who seem to have taken not unkindly to the French and the religion of the French priests. Parkman's "Jesuits in North America" tells thrillingly the story of the early missions among the Indians in Acadia of the Jesuits and Recollets, the latter a reformed branch of the Franciscan order. Under the influence of Father Peter Biard, a Jesuit at Port Royal, the aged chief of the Micmacs, Membertou, and many of his people were soon converted and this was the beginning of long, successful labor by missionaries of the Church of Rome among the Micmacs of Nova Scotia, the Malecites of New Brunswick, and the Abenakis of the country of the Kennebec. In 1663, Bishop Laval founded a seminary at Quebec, which soon become the centre of Jesuit missions on this continent; from Quebec priests were sent to Acadia, Illinois, and the lower Mississippi, Cape Breton Island being one of the chief missions. So vigorously were these missions pursued that by 1690, it is said, all the Micmacs had become Catholics.

The present diocese of Nova Scotia comprises the province of Nova Scotia (including Cape Breton) and Prince Edward Island, with ninety-four parishes sending delegates to the Diocesan Synod, and over a hundred names on the clergy list. In the beginning this diocese embraced all the British colonies in America from Newfoundland to Lake Superior, besides the islands of Bermuda. From it in 1793 was detached the second oldest Colonial diocese, the diocese of Quebec, then comprising the whole of Canada. In 1839 the see of Newfoundland, including Bermuda, was created, and in 1845 that of New Brunswick.

Three noteworthy epochs in the history of Nova Scotia must be kept in mind as one studies the history of the Church in this province, the period of the final cession of Acadia to England by the treaty of Utrecht in 1713, the founding of Halifax under Lord Cornwallis in 1749, and the Tory emigration from the revolting English colonies—chiefly New York and Massachusetts—between 1775 and 1784. The history of the Church does not properly go further back than the second of these periods, but for nearly forty years before that, in the garrison at Annapolis, English chaplains had ministered to the troops and the British or French settlers who lived about the fort.

When De Monts, in 1604, sailed into the tranquil bay, a century afterward named Annapolis Basin, he brought with him both a Huguenot minister and a Roman Catholic priest. Champlain was with the party, and he says that these reverend gentlemen agreed but poorly on the voyage, sometimes growing so fierce in their discussions that they fell to with their fists on questions of faith. "I leave you to judge," he naïvely says, "if it was a pleasant thing to see." In 1605 Port Royal was founded and is thus, save St. Augustine, in Florida, the oldest European settlement on the American continent. The early history of Annapolis Royal, which is still an important point in the diocese of Nova Scotia, perhaps exceeds in interest that of any town on the continent. There is, as has been said, a rare charm about the Nova Scotia scenery. It is true it has none of that semi-tropical luxuriance which makes the southern landscape, with its spreading palms, drooping cypresses, and rich odor-breathing magnolias, so attractive to the student of southern pioneer history, but there is a charm of outline, a virile grace in the landscape of Nova Scotia, a clearness in the skies, a vivid beauty in the forests, and a brilliancy in the wild flowers that in abundance come to bloom, that compensate for the lack of southern profusion. Its charms the adventurous noblemen, Champlain, De Monts, Poutrincourt, Pontgravé, and their associates felt as they sailed up the Annapolis Basin and anchored before the spot which soon became the site of their fort and their village. Their fort held no rude company, but such men as Marc Lescarbot, "avocat en Parlement," poet and first historian of the colony, and those other gallant sons of France who united to form the renowned brotherhood of *l'Ordre de Bon Temps*. After the first winter at Port Royal, its founders sailed away, but the houses were left standing, and in 1610 Poutrincourt came back with a new ship-load of French settlers who became the Pilgrim Fathers of the people of Acadia. On St. John Baptist's Day, in June, 1610, the priest La Flèche in his vestments, surrounded by gaily dressed French courtiers, soldiers in uniform, sailors, lawyers, laborers, and lackeys, baptized into Christianity on the shore of the basin twenty-one Indian converts, and to the reverent wonderment of the half-clad natives, in concert with his devout attendants, loud and clear, chanted the Church's Te Deum. As in Acadia generally so here for many years the spiritual welfare of the colonists and natives was in the hands of the Jesuit missionaries, of whom Father Biard was at least one of the most active and best known.

The conquest of Port Royal in 1710, which was the downfall of French authority in Acadia, was effected chiefly through the energy and persistency of the people of Massachusetts Bay. Naturally, the Puritans had no love for the French. Two peoples could not have been farther apart in temperament and general views of life than the New England people and the settlers of Acadia, and the dislike seems to have been mutual. The Indians, moreover, had in the beginning conceived a strong liking for the French, and had always taken sides with them against the English. Consequently there were frequent depredations of the Indians on the life and property of the New Eng-

and colonists, which only served to increase the hatred of New England to those who, as they believed, were inciting the Indians to deeds of violence. In 1710 the long-continued hostility resulted in an expedition against Port Royal, carefully planned between the colonies and the Home Government, with Colonel Francis Nicholson, as its chief leader, and Colonel Samuel Vetch as his associate. All the New England governors were instructed to aid the undertaking, and accordingly four regiments were raised in New England—two in Massachusetts, one in Connecticut, and one in New Hampshire and Rhode Island. Nicholson was general, and Vetch adjutant-general of the whole expedition, and the colonels of these New England regiments were Sir Charles Hobby, Tailer of Massachusetts, Whiting of Connecticut, and Shadrach Walton of New Hampshire. The grenadiers of Walton's regiment were commanded by Paul Mascarene, so long a prominent figure in the military government of Nova Scotia. On the 18th of September, the armament sailed from Nantasket, and early in October Monsieur de Subercase, the Governor of Port Royal, surrendered his fort and the English entered into final possession. The place was now named Annapolis Royal in honor of Queen Anne, and General Nicholson manned the newly acquired fort with two hundred marines and two hundred and fifty New England volunteers, commissioning Colonel Vetch as governor. Henceforth, instead of the white flag of the Bourbons, the red cross of St. George floated from the chief fort of Acadia as it had for so long floated over the neighboring New England shores.

At the annual meeting of the S. P. G., held February 20, 1712-13, it was resolved that the Honorable General Francis Nicholson then starting for America, Her Majesty's Governor of Nova Scotia or Acadia, and of Annapolis Royal, within the same province, and also commander of all Her Majesty's forces there and in Newfoundland in America; "should be requested to take cognizance of, and make inquiry concerning all the Society's missionaries, school-masters, and catechists; as also of the churches, glebes, parsonage houses and libraries, sent by the Society in the plantations within the verge of his commission (as a person who has deserved well of the Society in his several stations, for his love to the ministry, and for his laying the foundations of churches), accordingly a deputation has been given him under the common seal of the Society, for the purposes mentioned, with a salvo to the Queen's prerogative, and the jurisdiction of the Lord Bishop of London." Governor Nicholson, to whom the Venerable Society gave this trust, had no little influence upon the early history of the Church on the American continent. He is remarkable as having been governor of more colonies than any other Englishman. He was lieutenant-governor of New York under Edmund Andros from 1687 to 1689. He was governor of Virginia from 1690 to 1692, and again from 1699 to 1705, of Maryland from 1694 to 1699, of Nova Scotia from October 12, 1712, until August, 1717, and of South Carolina from 1721 to 1725. He served first in the army, and after commanding the expedition against Port Royal, went to England to urge the complete conquest of Canada, taking with him five Iroquois chiefs whom he presented to Queen Anne. The expedition against Canada was made, but was unsuccessful. Governor Nicholson was knighted in 1720, returned finally to England in June, 1725, and died in London, March 5, 1728. During his governorship of Virginia he helped secure a grant of twenty thousand acres of land for an endowment for William and Mary college in that churchly colony. While governor of Maryland he wrote the Archbishop of Canterbury that "unless bishops can be had the Church will surely decline," and in this colony he once led out of church a clergyman who was drunk, "and caned him soundly with his own hand."[1] From all the colonies he successively governed, he sent frequent letters to the S. P. G., informing them of the progress of the Church and making suggestions for the work of the Society. He was an energetic, but violent and unpopular man. In Maryland, "he hectored and browbeat a whole convocation and drove them to sign an adulatory testimony to his own religious devoutness." Commissary Blair, of Virginia, once wrote: "The governor rules us as if we were a company of galley slaves, by continual raving and thundering, cursing and swearing, base, abusive, Billingsgate language,

---

[1] McConnell's "History of the American Church," p. 89.

to that degree that it is utterly incredible."[1] One commissary was given the lie in his own house by the governor; and a correspondent of the Bishop of Litchfield, advocating to his lordship the appointment of a bishop for Virginia, writes that "if a right reverend father, of the stamp of Governor Nicholson, of Maryland, should come, it 'would make hell tremble.'"[2]

At the time of Nicholson's appointment to the governorship of Nova Scotia, the S. P. G. had in all America less than twenty missionaries and less than six lay schoolmasters. In 1716, in the report of the Society, a full list is given, and there we find in New York State seven clergymen, besides a catechist and an interpreter to Mr. Andrews, the Indian missionary; in New Jersey four clergymen, in South Carolina three, in North Carolina two, in Pennsylvania two, in Rhode Island two, and in Massachusetts two. In thirty years the list had so increased that in 1749, when the Cornwallis fleet sailed into Chebucto Bay, bringing two clergymen and one schoolmaster for Nova

---

[1] Bishop Perry: "Historical Collections," vol. Virginia, pp. 125, 491. [2] Ibid., p. 30.

Scotia, there were already working in America no less than sixty-three clergymen, twelve schoolmasters, and six catechists, of which number New England had nineteen clergymen, New York ten, South Carolina ten, Pennsylvania eight, New Jersey five, Georgia five, North Carolina two, Newfoundland two, and the Bahama Islands two.

This summary does not of course include the clergy of the self-supporting churches of Virginia and Maryland, where society was wealthier and more aristocratic than in the other colonies and where the Church had necessarily a firmer hold. In 1700, says McConnell,[1] "forty of the *less than three score* clergy scattered from Portsmouth to Charlestown were in these two colonies. There were in them two or three comfortable churches, built of imported brick. In every settlement was a church of logs with puncheon floors and clapboard roof. To these little log chapels the people came, on horseback and in canoes, from twenty, thirty, and forty miles away."

The first English chaplain at Annapolis Royal was Reverend John Harrison, for in

---

[1] "History of the American Church," p. 87.

Nicholson's journal we have this entry: "Tuesday the 10th (October, 1710), was solemnized a day of Thanksgiving for the success of Her Majesty's Arms in reducing Port Royal, etc., being so appointed by the General. After Divine Service which was performed in the Chapel by the Reverend Mr. John Harrison, Chaplain to Commodore Martin (and now left Chaplain to the Garrison by commission from the General) a sermon was preach'd by the Reverend Mr. Samuel Hesker, Chaplain to the Hon. Col. Reading's Marines."

Later he states that the Honorable General Nicholson was pleased to "Commissionate," before he went from Boston on the expedition to Port Royal, among other officers, "John Harrison, Clerk, Chaplain to the Garrison of Annapolis Royal." One of Mr. Harrison's early official acts, was the marriage of Magdelaine Maissonat, one of the original inhabitants, to William Winniett, a French Protestant, one of the captors of Port Royal, and an "officer of the fort."[1] It is also stated that he baptized their child, Anne Winniett, born March 20, 1712. Mr. Harrison was chaplain in 1720, for

---

[1] Murdoch, vol. i., p. 339.

that year, April 25th (o. s., May 6th, n. s.), Governor Philipps chose him as one of the first Councillors of the Province.[1] When other chaplains were appointed, he must still have lived at Annapolis, for November 23, 1732, he received from Governor Armstrong a grant of four acres, as church land, in the lower town, "measuring 660 feet, 407 feet, 605½ feet, and 274½ feet, on its external lines, its contents being four acres, three rods, and thirty-eight perches." It was granted free of quit rent, as glebe land, for the chaplain, or "if a parish be established," for the parish minister. It is probable that Mr. Harrison retained office as senior chaplain, but that as he grew older he needed assistance. At any rate, the Reverend Robert Cuthbert was chaplain as early as 1724, and as late as 1728, while, as we learn from the above record, Mr. Harrison was still there in November, 1732.

Reverend Robert Cuthbert was chaplain in 1724, for in that year he fell into disgrace in the garrison "for keeping company with Mrs. Margaret Douglass, wife of Alexander Douglass, contrary to his own promises, and the good

---

[1] Murdoch, vol. i., p. 363.

advice of his honor, the Lieutenant Governor," and Murdoch says, "contrary to all reproofs and admonitions from Alexander Douglass, her husband." The 22d of September, 1724, the Council ordered "that he, the said Mr. Robert Cuthbert, should be kept in the garrison without port liberty; and that his scandalous affair, and the satisfaction demanded by the injured husband, be transmitted, in order to be determined at home; and that the hon'ble. lieut. governor may write for another minister in his room." In 1728, this clergyman "was suspended from the exercise of his functions." In 1725, Mr. Cuthbert attempted to recover possession of a house which had been bought by Samuel Douglass from Lieutenant Jephson, of the 40th Regiment. This house, which had originally been built by Governor Vetch, and by him sold to Jephson in 1717, Cuthbert claimed as occupying a site on church lands.[1] The facts having appeared in evidence before the council, they gave Douglass leave to remove it.

Reverend Richard Watts was probably the

---

[1] Murdoch, vol. i., p. 420. Also Calnek's manuscript history of Annapolis, in King's College Library, Nova Scotia.

next chaplain, for July 20, 1732, he applied for, and by a deed dated September 19, 1733, we learn that he obtained, a grant of land.[1]

In 1728-29, he was in the pay of the S. P. G. as "schoolmaster at Annapolis Royal;" in 1730, he was one of sixteen witnesses to the oath of allegiance subscribed by two hundred and twenty-seven French "inhabitants of the Annapolis river," his name coming next to that of R. C. de Breslay, prêtre missionaire, curé, and being given, "Rich. Watts cler's."; and a deed has been found dated September 19, 1733, in which his name appears.

The first mention of missionaries or schoolmasters in Nova Scotia to be found in the reports of the S. P. G., is in the report presented at the annual meeting of the Society, held January 31, 1729. There we find the name of Mr. Watts, "Schoolmaster at Annapolis Royal," with a salary of £10 a year, and henceforth his name appears regularly in the reports of the Society, until the year 1738, when it is no longer found. August 8, 1737, the Reverend George Pigott at Marblehead, Massachusetts, writes that he had procured Mr. Watts to officiate at

---

[1] Murdoch, vol. i., p. 488.

his church, so that he could go to Providence to administer the Lord's Supper; and September 27, 1738, the Reverend Mr. Honeyman, senior missionary of the Society in Rhode Island, writes to England that not being well he had for some time had his church supplied by the Reverend Mr. Watts, "late the Society's schoolmaster at Annapolis Royal, and now settled in his neighborhood at Bristol." In 1768, Mr. Watts, or some one of his name, is reported as having acted for the previous year as schoolmaster at Windsor and Newport, Nova Scotia. He therefore left Nova Scotia in 1738, and Mr. Calnek, in his manuscript history of Annapolis, writing of the year 1742, says that there had been no chaplain to the garrison in the town since 1738, and the want of one was much felt and his absence deplored by those residents who needed his services.[1] This is probably ascertained from a letter to the Board of Trade from Mr. John Adams, a Boston trader, formerly resident at Annapolis, and for a little while president of the Council, who writes from Boston, March 12, 1742: "I would have returned to Annapolis before now,

---

[1] Calnek, Part 2, p. 3, and chapter 2, p. 17.

but there was no chaplain in the garrison to administer God's word and sacraments to the people; but the officers and soldiers in the garrison have profaned the holy sacraments of baptism and ministerial function, by presuming to baptize their own children. Why his majesty's chaplain does not come to his duty," he says, "I know not, but am persuaded it is a disservice and dishonor to our religion and nation; and as I have heard, some have got their children baptized by the Popish priests, for there has been no chaplain here for these four years."[1]

In 1744, during the siege of Annapolis by Indians, said to have been led on by the missionary, Monsieur de Loutre, the Church at Annapolis was burned, "through a mistake of orders." Other buildings also were pulled down at this time "as a measure of precaution and defence." It is doubtful if the Church was ever rebuilt.

In 1752, there was no chaplain at Annapolis, for the 15th of August, of that year, "a license was granted by the Governor to John Handfield, Esq., a justice of the Peace for the Province,

---

[1] Murdoch, vol. ii., p. 17.

to join together in holy wedlock Captain John Hamilton, widower, and Miss Mary Handfield, spinster, 'provided neither the chaplain of the garrison, nor any other lawful minister be present.'" Captain Handfield, to whom this authority was given, was then commanding officer at Annapolis, and was, in 1755, engaged in the expulsion of the Acadians. Captain John Hamilton was a son of Major Otho Hamilton of the 40th Regiment, of the Hamiltons of Olivestob, East Lothian, Scotland. Captain Hamilton had some time before been made a prisoner by the Indians and taken to Quebec, but had lately been ransomed.

In 1749, the government was transferred to the newly-founded settlement at Halifax, although a few troops were kept at Annapolis until somewhere about 1850.

In early times, before Halifax was founded, one other military post in Nova Scotia besides Annapolis for a time came under the eye of the S. P. G. That point was Canso, where from 1736 until 1743, at a salary of £10 a year, a certain Mr. Peden was continuously kept as schoolmaster. In 1725, there were forty-nine English families at Canso and "only one or two" at Annapolis, and Governor Armstrong thought the seat of government should be removed to Canso, but whether at this or any other time there was an English chaplain stationed there, is not known. The place was captured by M. Du Vivier with a few armed vessels and about nine hundred men from Louisburg, in May, 1744, and the seventy or eighty soldiers and few inhabitants there, taken as prisoners to Louisburg and afterward sent to Boston. After Mr. Peden's removal, which was probably at the time of Du Vivier's capture of the place, we find no mention of Canso in the Society's reports.

CHAPTER II.

HALIFAX AND THE VENERABLE SOCIETY.

THE scheme for founding a settlement on Chebucto Bay is said to have originated with the people of Massachusetts, who, calling the attention of the Home Government to the claims and encroachments of the French on this part of the continent, and the consequent insecurity of its possessions in Acadia, at the same time suggested that the establishment of a trading post here would be of great commercial benefit. The Lords of Trade and Plantations took the matter up, and the government soon issued a proclamation offering to men of all ranks discharged from the army and navy, and to a certain number of mechanics and farmers, who would emigrate, a free passage to Nova Scotia, subsistence for a year after landing, arms, ammunition and utensils, free grants of land in the province and a civil government, with all the privileges enjoyed in the other English colonies. To this proclamation so many responded that early in May two thousand four hundred and seventy-six persons under command of the Honorable Edward Cornwallis, M.P.,[1] as captain-general and governor of Nova Scotia, in thirteen transports and a sloop of war set sail. Over fifteen hundred of these settlers were men, and over five hundred men-of-war sailors. In June the fleet sailed into Halifax harbor, a magnificent sheet of water where the navies of the world might safely ride, and on the fourteenth of that month on board one of the transports—the "Beaufort" —a civil government was organized with Colonel Paul Mascarene, Captain Edward Howe, Captain John Goreham, Messrs. Benjamin Green, John Salisbury, and Hugh Davidson as

---

[1] The Hon. Edward, afterward Lord Cornwallis, was the fifth son of Charles, third Baron Cornwallis, by Lady Charlotte Butler, daughter of Richard, Earl of Arran, uncle to the celebrated Duke of Ormonde. He was born February 22, 1713, was M.P. for the borough of Eye in 1749, and in 1753, shortly after his return from Halifax, was elected for the city of Westminster. He married the same year a daughter of Lord Townshende, but left no family. In 1759 he was made a major-general, and was afterward governor of Gibraltar. General Cornwallis was brother of Dr. Frederic Cornwallis, Archbishop of Canterbury, and uncle to the Lord Cornwallis who defeated General Gates at Camden, South Carolina, in 1780, and afterward surrendered at Yorktown to General Washington.

councillors. The first four of these were from the garrison at Annapolis, the last two were probably members of His Excellency's suite. The name Halifax was given the new settlement in compliment to George Montague, Earl of Halifax, then at the head of the Board of Trade.

The old part of the city of Halifax is built on the ascent of a hill, and slopes gently from the harbor to the commanding citadel, which overlooks and guards the town. On this high hill the settlers naturally built their block house, while all about the green slope, from Buckingham Street on the north to Salter Street on the south, they scattered their log and tent dwellings, replacing these as soon as they were able with frame houses, the materials for which were brought from Massachusetts Bay. In August, 1750, three hundred and fifty more settlers arrived in the ship "Alderney," and in September, three hundred German Protestants from the Palatinate in the ship "Anne." In 1751 and 1752, over a thousand more came, and these German people formed an almost distinct town by themselves in the north part of the city, where they built a little Lutheran church which still stands—the quaintest building in Halifax—to which later generations have facetiously given the name of the "Chicken-Cock" church, from the rather disproportionate size of the cock on the top of its little spire. These people were chiefly Lutherans, and after a few years they moved farther west along the coast, to what is now Lunenburg, where, under the influence of the S. P. G. missionaries, many of them came into the Church of England, the little church they had built in Halifax also becoming Church of England property.

Thus began this quaint English-looking city, with one of the finest harbors in the world, and an ancient citadel, where flags are always flying, and regimental guards pacing their daily or nightly rounds. Halifax is superbly located. Its glorious harbor, in which the fleets of the world might safely anchor, opens westward into Bedford Basin, the scenery around which is of rare beauty. About a mile and a half west of the town one finds the almost equally picturesque North-west Arm, along which lie many beautiful residences. About seven miles north of the centre of the city, near the head of Bedford Basin, is a beautiful spot, now much used as a picnic ground, which every Haligonian knows as "the Prince's Lodge." It is part of the estate in old times leased by Sir John Wentworth to the Duke of Kent for his royal residence during the seven years that that prince, the father of Queen Victoria, lived in Nova Scotia. Sir John Wentworth had his country mansion there, and called it, in allusion to "Romeo and Juliet," "Friar Laurence's Cell." The Duke enlarged the original house until it was a fine two-storied villa, somewhat in the Italian style, with extensive wings at the north and south and a great hall and drawing-rooms in the centre. Back of the house were stables for his horses, and the grounds, though rustic, and having all the marks that nature had originally put upon them, contained many charming surprises. His Royal Highness, who was at this time commander of all the forces in North America, had a signal apparatus on an adjoining hill, by means of which he could send his orders to the citadel in town. In 1800 the Duke of Kent began the erection of the present citadel in Halifax, first removing the old insecure fortifications, and then building the massive walls that now inclose the fort. A conspicuous monument of his Royal Highness, still remaining, is the square wooden clock tower below the glacis, directly above the middle of the town. At the north end of the city lies the dock-yard, with its half-mile of water-front, the foundations of which were laid in 1788. Within its wall of solid masonry are the commissioner's residence, and the houses of other employees, whose official duties include the landing and shipping of naval stores. At the extreme north of the dock-yard is Admiralty House, where the naval commander lives from May till October, when the war ships move to Bermuda, Nassau, or Jamaica for the winter. There is hardly a week all summer long when more than one war ship of the fleet is not flying its flag in the harbor, hardly an evening when the music of some magnificently trained ship's band is not floating from mid-stream to the Halifax and Dartmouth shores. Not far from Admiralty House, high above the harbor, rise the naval and military hospitals, the Wellington Barracks, and the huge garrison chapel, where every Sunday hundreds of soldiers sing and pray.

Halifax was re-founded in the days of the American Revolution, in March, 1776, when, the British fleet having evacuated Boston, ten thousand people sought the little town, and in 1783, when more than thirty thousand Loyalists took refuge in the British maritime provinces. On its social side the Revolution was in great part the revolt of democracy against aristocracy, and this tide of Tory emigration swept into Nova Scotia a positive sympathy with England, strong aristocratic feeling, and a distaste for republican government that have never essentially weakened. A large number of these Loyalists, many of whom were people of the highest culture, and who had held leading positions in the revolting colonies, received grants of land in the large unsettled province of New Brunswick, hitherto part of Nova Scotia, but many remained in the latter province, on whose southern shore they founded, with great ceremony and high hopes, the little town of Shelburne. By this means the population of Halifax rose in six or seven years from three to twelve thousand, and so influential, and in the cases of some who left the United States before their goods were confiscated, so rich were these new citizens, that no little jealousy was aroused on the part of the old inhabitants, especially when they found them monopolizing all the leading offices in the gift of the crown. It was at this time that Government House was built, the fine stone mansion on Pleasant Street, where many successive royal governors have held their stately little courts. The house is an exact reproduction of the famous Lansdowne House in London, and the first governor to live in it was Sir John Wentworth, who before the Revolution was governor of New Hampshire, and while governor of Nova Scotia received the honor of a baronetcy. Besides Government House, there are two buildings in Halifax that have great historic interest. One of these is the Province Building, where the Provincial Legislature in both its branches meets; the other, St. Paul's Church, which contains more mural tablets and escutcheons than any church on the continent, not even excepting the old cathedral at Quebec. The Province Building was begun in 1811, and finished in 1819. Here in the legislative council-chamber is the only noteworthy collection of paintings Halifax

Halifax and the Venerable Society. 33

owns, the finest of them being a portrait, by Benjamin West, of Chief-Justice Strange, in a scarlet robe and wig. Of St. Paul's Church and the parish that built it we shall have much more to say.

The work of the Society for the Propagation of the Gospel, in Nova Scotia, begins with the founding of Halifax by Lord Cornwallis. The Society's report for 1748 states, that: "Upon an application from the Lords Commissioners for Trade and Plantations the Society hath agreed to send over to the new Colony of *Nova Scotia*, as soon as Settlements are made and the Occasions of the Colony require, six Missionaries and six School-masters at a very large Expense, and even beyond their present Ability, for the Support of Religion in that Infant Colony, and to prevent the first Settlers from being perverted to Popery, there being a great Number of Priests residing among the present Inhabitants, who are mostly French Papists and under the Direction of the French Bishop of Quebeck." In pursuance of this agreement the Venerable Society sent with the Cornwallis fleet to Halifax, two clergymen, the Reverend William Tutty and the Reverend William

Anwell, and a schoolmaster, Mr. Edward Halhead, the clergymen to receive the usual stipend of seventy pounds a year each, the schoolmaster a salary of fifteen pounds. Of these two clergymen, the Reverend William Tutty is known to have been educated at Emmanuel College, Cambridge, but of the antecedents of the Reverend William Anwell, no record has been preserved in Nova Scotia. In the report of the Society presented in 1750, it is stated that " Mr. Tutty is happily fixed as minister in the first settlement, viz., in the town of Halifax, which is already become populous, and that he behaves very properly and is very useful in his station; but the Society being not so well-satisfied with the conduct of Mr. Anwyll, they have recalled him from Nova Scotia; and have appointed the Reverend Mr. Moreau, a worthy clergyman of French extraction, to be their missionary to a settlement now forming, which is chiefly to be composed of French Protestants." Mr. Anwell, though removed from his post, did not return to England, as the St. Paul's parish register states that "William Aynwell, clerk, late missionary, was buried, February 10, 1749-50." Mr. Tutty, in 1753, went back to

England to attend to some private affairs, and while there fell ill and died. In the report of the Society for 1754, it is recorded, that "the new settlers in Nova Scotia have suffered a great loss this year in the death of the Reverend Mr. Tutty, the Society's worthy missionary to them, and to supply it in some measure, the Society hath approved of the removal of the Reverend Mr. Wood, from New Brunswick, in New Jersey, to this colony, and appointed him missionary in it." Mr. Halhead's name appears for the last time in the report of the Society for 1752.

In 1749 the nearest Episcopal church to Halifax was Queen's Chapel, Portsmouth, New Hampshire, of which the Reverend Arthur Browne was rector. In Boston Dr. Timothy Cutler was the minister of Christ Church, and Dr. Henry Caner rector of King's Chapel. At St. Paul's, Newburyport, Reverend Matthias Plant was minister, and at St. Michael's, Marblehead, Reverend Mr. Malcolm. Stratford, Connecticut, had Dr. Samuel Johnson as its minister, and Trinity Church, Newport, Reverend James Honeyman, while Trinity Church, New York, had as rector the Reverend Henry

Barclay. The little church colony in Maine, "Gorge's ever faithful settlement on the Kennebec," of which McConnell writes that "through all the years they had held steadfastly to their Church and Prayer Book," had been without a minister since the Reverend Robert Jordan was driven away in 1675, and did not have one until 1756. Its first church was organized at Pownalboro, June 19, 1760, and Reverend Jacob Bailey, who labored also at Frankfort, and occasionally at George Town, Brunswick, Harpswell, and Richmond, and a few years later with so many other Loyalists took refuge in Nova Scotia, was its minister.

The origin of Halifax being what we have described it, we shall naturally expect to find the Church of England taking the highest place in the people's life. The old inhabitants were not by any means all Churchmen: there were among them not a few Roman Catholics and New England Congregationalists, but as we shall presently see, the Church of England was, as a rule, the church of the governing class, the officers of the army and navy, and when the American Revolution drove them here, of the New York and New England Tories, who thronged the older settlements of the sparsely populated province, and in the Nova Scotia wilds built themselves new towns. Before we trace more fully, however, the history of the Church in Halifax, we must examine the legal standing given it in the newly organized colony.

CHAPTER III.

THE CHURCH ESTABLISHED.

In 1758 the first assembly of the province met, and the question of religion was of course one of the first to be considered. This assembly was composed of nineteen members, six of whom ranked as *esquires*, thirteen as *gentlemen*. A large proportion of them were men born in Great Britain, a few were of Puritan stock, born in the New England colonies, and one at least was of German origin. When we remember that three years before, the provincial authorities, seconded by the home government, had resorted to the extreme measure of the expulsion of the Acadians, and that that step had been made necessary, as was thought, by the active and long-continued hostility of Roman Catholic priests to English and Protestant rule, we shall not be surprised to find the first act regarding religion passed in the province, an act not only for the establishment of religion, but also for *the suppression of Popery*. From such an assembly, however, as that convened in

Halifax in 1758, representing a population already considerably differing in faith, and now beginning to look toward Congregational New England for settlers for the lands of the exiled Acadians and for the enlargement of the trading and fishing settlements on the western shores, we shall not expect rigid laws in favor of the Church of England. The day for uniformity acts in the colonies, such as had been passed in Virginia in 1631-32, and in Maryland seventy years later, had now gone by, and toleration of Dissent was recognized, not only as expedient, but as the undoubted right of Dissenters themselves. Consequently, while the provisions of the act of this Nova Scotia Assembly are severe against Roman Catholics, they are correspondingly lenient toward all Protestant Dissenters of whatever name. The act of the thirty-second year of George II., passed by the first assembly, is as follows:

CAP. V.

An Act for the establishment of religious public Worship in this Province, and for suppressing Popery.

Forasmuch *as His Majesty upon the settlement of the Province, was pleased, in His pious concern for the advancement of God's glory, and the more decent celebration of the divine ordinances amongst us, to erect a Church for religious worship, according to the usuage of the Church of England; in humble imitation of his Royal example, and for the more effectual attainment of his Majesty's pious intentions, that we might in the exercise of religious duties, be seeking for the divine favour and protection, be it therefor enacted by his Excellency the Governor, Council and Assembly,* That the sacred rites and ceremonies of divine worship, according to the liturgy of the Church established by the laws of England, shall be deemed the fixed form of worship amongst us, and the place wherein such liturgy shall be used, shall be respected and known by the name of the Church of England as by law established. And that for the preservation of purity and unity of doctrine and discipline in the church, and the right administration of the sacraments, no minister shall be admitted to officiate as a minister of the Church of England, but such as shall produce to the Governor, a testimonial, that he hath been licenced by the Bishop of London, and shall publickly declare his assent and consent to the book of common prayer, and shall subscribe to be conformable to the orders and constitutions of the Church of England, and the laws there established; upon which the Governor is hereby requested to induct the said minister into any parish that shall make presentation of him. And if any other person presenting himself a minister of the Church of England, shall, contrary to this act, presume to teach or preach publicly or privately, the Governor and Council are hereby desired and empowered to suspend and silence the person so offending.

II. *Provided nevertheless*, and it is the true intent and meaning of this act, that Protestants, dissenting from the Church of England, whether they be Calvinists, Lutherans, Quakers, or under what denomination soever, shall have free liberty of conscience, and may erect and build meeting houses for public worship, and may choose and elect ministers for the carrying on divine service and administration of the sacraments, according to their several opinions; and all contracts made between their ministers and their congregations for the support of the ministry, are hereby declared valid, and shall have their full force and effect, according to the tenor and conditions thereof; and all such Dissenters shall be excused from any rates or taxes to be made and levied for the support of the established Church of England.

III. *And be it further enacted*, That every popish person, exercising any ecclesiastical jurisdiction, and every popish priest or person exercising the function of a popish priest, shall depart out of this province on or before the twenty-fifth day of March, 1759. And if any such person or persons shall be found in this province after the said day, he or they shall, upon conviction, be adjudged to suffer perpetual imprisonment: and if any person or persons so imprisoned, shall escape out of prison he or they shall be deemed and adjudged guilty of felony without benefit of clergy.

IV. *And be it further enacted*, That any persons, who shall knowingly harbour, relieve, conceal, or entertain any such clergyman of the popish religion, or popish priest, or persons exercising the functions of a popish priest, shall forfeit fifty pounds, one moiety to his Majesty for the support of his government in this province, and the other moiety to the informer, and shall also be adjudged to be set in the pillory, and to find sureties for his good behaviour at the discretion of the court.

V. *And be it enacted*, That every offence against this act, shall and may be inquired of, heard and determined, at his Majesty's Supreme Court of Assize, and General Gaol Delivery, or by a special commission of Oyer and Terminer.

VI. *And be it further enacted*, That it shall and may be lawful for any justice of the peace, upon information by oath, or any reasonable cause of suspicion, to issue his warrant for apprehending any such popish ecclesiastical person, popish priest or person exercising the function of a popish priest, or any persons knowingly harbouring, relieving, concealing or entertaining them or any of them, and to commit any such person or persons respectively, who shall so offend against this act, to his Majesty's gaol, for trial as aforesaid, and to require sureties for the appearance of the witness or witnesses, against any offender or offenders upon such trial; and to make return of his proceedings to such court on the information of such witnesses, and the examination of any offender or offenders.

VII. *Provided nevertheless*, That this Act shall not extend, or be construed to extend to any such Romish ecclesiastical persons, who shall be sent into the province as prisoners of war, or who shall by shipwreck or any other distress or necessity, be driven into the province, so as that such prisoners of war do not escape before they can be sent out of the province, or that such persons arriving through necessity as aforesaid, depart out of the province as soon as there may be opportunity; and that they also forthwith after their arrival, attend the Governor or Commander-in-Chief of the province for the time being, if near the place of his residence, or otherwise a justice of the peace, and represent the necessity of their arrival, and obey such directions as the said Governor, Commander in Chief or Justice shall give them for their departure; and so as that neither the said prisoners of war, nor the said persons arriving through such necessity, shall exercise any ecclesiastical jurisdiction, or any part of the function of a popish priest, during his or their abode in the province, in which case he or they shall be liable to the penalties of this Act.

The fierce enactment of the first provincial assembly against the Roman Catholic worship, must soon have caused dissatisfaction, for it is certain that there were always members of that church sprinkled among the Protestants in Halifax and the adjacent settlements. For twenty-five years, however, no Roman Catholic church was established in the province; but at last, in 1783, the law was repealed, and the next year, on Monday, July 19, 1784, "in presence of a great concourse of gentlemen and other people" the frame of a church was raised in Halifax, near the site of the present St. Mary's Cathedral. "Test oaths against popery," however, were required from all candidates for office until 1827, in the early part of which year, the Reverend John Carrol and other Roman Catholics made a strong and successful petition to the house of assembly that the Test Act should be abolished. In this petition, the original of which is said to have been in the handwriting of Lawrence O'Connor Doyle, the Roman Catholics say that the tests are based on a misunderstanding of their tenets and impute to them practices which their souls abhor: "We do not adore the saints," they say; "but we pray to them. We know they possess no inherent power; but that they feel an interest in us. Even this present petition will illustrate this Tenet; in it we pray your Honorable House to *intercede* with his Majesty, though you have none of his authority; so we solicit the saints to interpose with Christ, though they have nothing of his Divinity; as then we can pray for the intercession of your Honorable House without an insult to your Sovereign, so we pray for the intercession of the Saints without an offence to our God." "The Mass," they add, "is the principal rite of our Church. In it we adore none but God. He told us he gave us his body. We only believe that he meant what he said."

The speeches in the house on receipt of this petition were perhaps among the finest ever made in the provincial legislature. The assembly contained such men as Samuel George William Archibald, Thomas Chandler Haliburton, Richard John Uniacke, and Charles Rufus Fairbanks, men of great dignity of presence, marked power of mind, and fine oratorical ability. The most telling speeches were made by Richard John Uniacke, and Thomas Chandler Haliburton. Mr. Haliburton said that, in England since the Protestant Reformation it had been thought necessary to impose test oaths, lest the Catholics, who were the most numerous body, might restore the ancient order of things, and particularly as there was danger of a Catholic succession; but when the Stuart race became extinct, the test oaths should have been buried with the last of that unfortunate family. Whatever might be the effect of emancipation in Great Britain, here there was not the slightest pretension for continuing restrictions; for if the whole house and all the council were Catholics, it would be impossible to alter the constitution—the governor was appointed by the king, and not by the people, and no act could pass without his consent. "Every man," said he, "who lays his hand on the New Testament, and says that is his book of faith, whether he be Catholic or Protestant, Churchman or dissenter, Baptist or Methodist, however much we may differ in doctrinal points, he is my brother, and I embrace him. We all travel by different roads to the same God." Mr. Uniacke also said eloquently: "Far be it from me to disparage the creed of others; no, in my opinion, the humblest clergyman in the humblest church of the humblest congregation, if he practises the precepts of his God—if he conforms to the rules of morality, that man is, in my conviction, an object as pleasing to Heaven as he who wears the richest mitre in the proudest cathedral of Europe." It may be said here, that the Roman Catholicism of Nova Scotia has usually been of a mild and conciliatory character, and that there has been the freest social intercourse, especially in Halifax, between Roman Catholics and Protestants.

In 1812 some attempt was clearly made to get a law passed by the assembly to exact support for the Church of England from the people at large, for in April of that year, the house resolved to address the governor to the effect that, "as the inhabitants of this colony are composed of persons professing various religious sentiments, all of whom, since the first settlement of this province, have been exempt from yielding any support to the Church of England, except such as profess to be members of that Church, the house of assembly, anxiously desirous of preserving harmony among all denominations of Christians, cannot agree to make provision for the clergy of the Church of England out of the public treasury, or in any way raise money by taxes on other classes of Christians for the support of that Church."

The first provincial assembly also passed a law restricting marriage by license, without the publication of banns, to clergymen of the Church of England. The Church of England Prayer Book prescribes that banns of marriage shall be published on three successive Sundays, but the law also allowed speedier and more private marriages than the publication of banns admitted of, by means of licenses obtained from the proper authorities. The law in Nova

The Church Established.   49

Scotia was similar to that in England and Scotland.[1] Neither English Dissenters, nor ministers of the Scotch Church were allowed to obtain licenses directly. The law concerning marriage by license specified that licenses should be granted only to clergymen of the

---

[1] 32 GEO. II, CAP. XVII., 1758.

Be it enacted by His Excellency the Governor, Council and Assembly, and by the authority of the same it is hereby enacted, That any person presuming to officiate in solemnizing any marriage, before notice of the parties' intention of marriage shall be publicly given, on three several Sundays, or holy days, in time of divine service, in some congregation within the town or towns, where each of the parties do reside, or for which marriage license shall not have been obtained, under the hand of the Governor or Commander in Chief of the Province for the time being, shall forfeit and pay to the use of His Majesty's government, fifty pounds, to be recovered by bill, plaint, or information in any of the Courts of Record within this Province.

II. *And be it further enacted,* That if any clergyman, officiating as such, in any congregation in the town or towns, where the parties reside, shall neglect or refuse to make, or cause to be made, such publication, when thereunto reasonably requested, he shall forfeit the sum of fifty pounds, to be recovered in manner aforesaid: and be subject nevertheless to an action of damages, to be brought by any of the parties aggrieved.

III. *And be it further enacted,* That if any clergyman shall refuse to marry any persons requesting him thereto, and making known to him that they have been duly published, or have obtained a license as aforesaid, he shall forfeit the sum of fifty pounds, to be recovered in manner aforesaid, and be subject to the like action of damages.

Established Church, and should not be performed except with the use of the marriage service of the Book of Common Prayer. This restriction seems early to have caused dissatisfaction, and for a long time was in many places practically a dead letter. In 1800, Sir John Wentworth, who casually speaks of his long-continued devotion to the interests of the Church of England, complains to Mr. King, under secretary of state, that Mr. Stanser of St. Paul's, was in the habit of receiving marriage licenses, and transferring them to Roman Catholic, Presbyterian, and Methodist clergyman, receiving the fees, himself. This was a clever way of evading an unjust law, and was undoubtedly common in other parts of the province besides Halifax. That part of the law which prescribed the use of the Prayer Book was in such cases, probably, wholly ignored.

In 1818 the Dissenters petitioned the house to have these restrictions abolished. The issuing of licenses to Church clergymen alone, they alleged, was an infringement of their legal rights. The gentlemen who spoke on behalf of the Dissenters in the house of assembly declared warmly that in their opinion it was a grievance that Dissenters were obliged to ask for licenses to marry, from the head of a church to which they did not belong. After considerable discussion the house resolved that "His Excellency the Lieutenant Governor be requested (in case he shall consider himself authorized by law to do so), to grant licenses to clergymen dissenting from the Church of England, authorizing them to celebrate marriages, pursuant to the rites and ceremonies of their respective churches; and that Mr. Speaker do deliver the foregoing resolution to His Excellency." The next year a joint address of both houses to the lieutenant governor, respecting marriage licenses, containing their reasons for passing this bill, was adopted, in order that the lieutenant governor might communicate its statements to His Majesty's ministers. A little later, however, Earl Bathurst writes to the governor, Lord Dalhousie, disallowing the new act, and giving his reasons at length. He considers that the right to marry by banns is all that Dissenters can properly ask, as marriage by license is not in use among them, and is, on the whole, disapproved of by the English Church as tending to irregularity. He wishes any such bill to be rejected by the governor.

Early in this century the statute restricting marriage licenses to Church of England clergymen with any other statutes discriminating against Dissenters, was finally abolished, and since that time, whatever pre-eminence the Church may have had in Nova Scotia, has been not legal but prescriptive, the result of her ancient traditions and the superiority of her organization and methods. Numerically, as we shall see in the chapter on other religious bodies, the Church of England has long stood only fourth among the religious denominations of the province.

CHAPTER IV.
HISTORIC ST. PAUL'S.

ONE of the first acts of the surveyors who planned the town of Halifax, was to lay out the site of a church, and among the first buildings, for the frames of which orders were sent to Massachusetts, was the venerable structure that stands in the centre of the town opposite the Grand Parade, known as St. Paul's, the Mother Church of the diocese of Nova Scotia. In a letter dated March 19, 1750, Governor Cornwallis says: "I expect the frame of the church will be here next month from New England. The plan is the same with that of Marybone (Marylebone) Chapel." A few months later he writes that the church then setting up will cost a thousand pounds by the estimate sent from Boston. Whoever was its architect, and whether the church was a copy of Marylebone Chapel or not, it has always been claimed that in its original form it was identical even to the size of the panes of glass with St. Peter's, Vere St., London, and we have

Bishop John Inglis, the third bishop of Nova Scotia, as authority for the statement that the plans used in building it were the same as those used in building St. Peter's. The church, though not finished, was formally opened for divine service by the Reverend William Tutty, September 2, 1750,[1] and in a letter of this clergyman's to the Society, written October 29th, he says that the church when completed will be a very handsome structure. From 1750 to 1752 over two thousand Germans were added to the population of Halifax, and under the tuition of Mr. Burger, a German Swiss minister who came with them, Mr. Tutty devoted himself to studying their language in which he made such progress that he was soon able to minister to these people in their own tongue. After a time this Mr. Burger went to England for Episcopal ordination which he obtained, afterward starting for Halifax with a large number of German Bibles and Prayer Books for the use of his congregation.[2] Nothing more, how-

---

[1] St. Paul's will thus, September 2, 1892, have completed the one hundred and forty-second year since its formal opening for divine worship.

[2] In 1750, as also frequently afterward, the S.P.G., in connection with the S.P.C.K. sent out to Nova Scotia, a generous supply of Bibles and Prayer Books, in French and English.

ever, is heard of him and it is probable that the vessel in which he sailed was lost on the voyage.

In 1752, the Reverend John Breynton, who had been a chaplain on one of His Majesty's ships of war during the siege of Louisburg, was sent out to assist Mr. Tutty, and the latter soon obtained leave of absence to go to England on some private business. While there, in 1754, he died, and the Society, appointing Mr. Breynton to the charge of the Halifax mission, permitted the Reverend Thomas Wood to remove from New Jersey, where he had been the Society's missionary at New Brunswick and Elizabethtown, to Nova Scotia to share this clergyman's work. In the autumn of 1752 Mr. Breynton wrote that Mr. Wood had given him very seasonable help all the preceding winter, but was then gone to Annapolis by the Governor's order.

In October, 1750, Mr. Tutty had written that the number of inhabitants not including the soldiery was then four thousand, but notwithstanding the arrival of so many Germans and others in the mean time, in December, 1755, Mr. Breynton writes that the population of

Halifax, through the starting of other settlements, has fallen to thirteen hundred, eight hundred of whom profess themselves members of the Church of England. The church, he says, is now "completely finished without and makes a very handsome appearance, and it is aisled and plastered within and pewed after a rough manner by the inhabitants." During the year he had baptized a hundred and seveny-three children and two adults, and at that time his communicant list numbered ninety.

The parish of St. Paul's was organized with clearly drawn boundary lines and a corporate body of wardens and vestrymen in 1759. In the autumn of that year the first vestry meeting was held, on which occasion the ordinary English way of appointing church wardens was followed, the clergyman nominating one, the parishioners the other. At a meeting of the corporation, held April 7th of the following year, a sum of thirty pounds was assessed on the members of the parish for providing church elements, paying for surplices, and fencing in the new burying ground. In a joint letter of Messrs. Breynton and Wood, of December, 1760, these clergymen write: "The church at

Halifax (called St. Paul's) is almost finished in a neat and elegant manner; and the Province laws in regard to the establishment of religion are as favorable to the Church of England as the circumstances of the colony will admit; and there will be at least five thousand persons in the out settlements this year, most of whom we have reason to believe would profess themselves members of our church, provided pious and prudent missionaries should be settled among them; and in the mean time, we promise to make it our constant endeavor to establish peace and unanimity among them, and to extend our mission as far as possible, having nothing so much at heart as the furtherance of our most holy religion, and approving ourselves worthy of the great trust reposed in us."

In 1764, Mr. Wood, with the consent of the vestry and the leave of Governor Wilmot, removed to Annapolis, leaving Mr. Breynton in sole charge of Halifax, the population of which numbered still but thirteen hundred. The clergyman's labor must, however, have been very severe, for there were in the town, besides the regular inhabitants, five hundred of the army and seven hundred of the navy, who were professed members of the Church of England. Of Mr. Breynton's goodness and faithfulness too much cannot be said. His friend, Jonathan Belcher, the first Chief Justice of Nova Scotia, who never loses an opportunity of praising him, calls him a man of "indefatigable labors," "experienced assiduity," "moderation," and "perfect good acceptance," and what we know of his ministry seems such as entirely to justify even stronger praise than these epithets express. His interest in not only the mixed population he found in his new cure, but the ignorant and squalid Micmacs of the Nova Scotia woods, his hearty God-speed to all of whatever name whom he found trying to do good to men, his solicitude for the unhappy Loyalists, who at the time of the Revolution thronged the little town, and especially for those clergymen who came to him from New England, homeless and destitute, stamps him the true priest, set apart not only by the hands of bishops but by the gentle Spirit of the living God. Dr. Hill says of him, "He was the personal friend and counsellor of the successive Governors and Lieutenant Governors, the associate and adviser of all others in authority, the friend and helper of the poor, the sick and afflicted, and the promoter and supervisor of education. He doubtless deserved the high encomium passed upon him during his absence by a brother missionary, the Reverend William Bennett, that 'he never knew a man so universally regretted by every individual of every denomination.'" While in England, in 1771, Mr. Breynton received the degree of Doctor of Divinity. In 1785, sometime before September, he sailed for England, leaving the Reverend Joshua Wingate Weeks in charge of the parish. Neither he nor the parish seems to have expected that he would not return, but for some reason he found it inexpedient to do so. After four years he resigned and the Reverend Robert Stanser, who later became the second Bishop of the Diocese, was appointed in England to the vacant rectorship, in June, 1789, sailing from Portsmouth to assume the charge. The successive rectors of St. Paul's since Dr. Stanser's time have been the Reverend John Inglis, who became rector in 1816, on the elevation of Dr. Stanser to the episcopate, the Reverend Robert Willis, elected in 1824, soon after Dr. Inglis was made Bishop, the Reverend George W. Hill, D.C.L., who became rector in 1865, the Reverend Charles Hole, who succeeded Dr. Hill in 1886, and the seventh rector, the Reverend Dyson Hague, inducted into the rectorship in 1890. In its history the church building has undergone several changes. In 1786, a large amount of money was expended on the interior of the building, the governor's pew also being "ornamented with a canopy and King's arms." In 1795, the church was railed in by the Duke of Kent, who was then residing in Halifax, and in 1812 an addition of twelve feet was made at the northern or entrance end, and a chime of three bells was presented by Mr. Andrew Belcher, son of Chief Justice, and father of Rear-Admiral Sir Edward Belcher, K.C.B. In 1868, wings were added to the church, and in 1872, a chancel was built.

From the close connection of St. Paul's parish with the Nova Scotia government, and with the public affairs of the province, important services have from time to time been held in this historic church. On Monday, October 2, 1753, Jonathan Belcher, second son of Governor Jonathan Belcher, of Massachusetts, was sworn the first Chief Justice of Nova Scotia, and after a stately reception and "an elegant breakfast at the "Great Pontac," a noted hotel of the period, in his scarlet robes, accompanied by Lieutenant-Governor Lawrence and many other public and private citizens, proceeded with the commission carried before him to the church, where the Reverend Dr. Breynton preached a sermon from the text: "I am one of them that are peaceable and faithful in Israel."

On Tuesday, February 17, 1761, at eleven o'clock, the president and members of the Council, officers of the army, and chief inhabitants, dressed in mourning, went in procession from Government House to St. Paul's Church, where the Reverend Thomas Wood preached a funeral sermon on the death of King George the Second. The pulpit, reading desk and governor's pew were hung with black, minute guns were fired from the batteries; the guns continued firing for an hour and a half, and the flags from the citadel and George's Island were at half-mast all day, all amusements being prohibited for a month, as part of the public mourning.

In July, 1766, the Rev. Mr. Wood, having

sufficiently studied the Micmac language, read prayers in that tongue in St. Paul's in the presence of a number of Indians as well as the Governor, Lord William Campbell, Colonel Dalrymple, and most of the officers of the Army and Navy and the leading citizens. Before the service the Indians sang an anthem, and then a Micmac chief came forward and kneeling down prayed that God would bless His Majesty, King George the Third, "their lawful King and governor," and when he rose up Mr. Wood at his desire, explained his prayer in English to the congregation. The natives then sang another anthem, and when all was done "thanked God, the Governor and Mr. Wood for the opportunity they had had of hearing prayer in their own language."

St. Paul's church contains more mural tablets and escutcheons than even the cathedral at Quebec. No less than fifty tablets line its walls and to the pilasters are attached eight hatchments. The first person known to have been buried in the vaults beneath it was Colonel Charles Lawrence, governor of the province during those important events, the expulsion of the Acadians, and the re-settling of their lands by Puritans from the New England States. To show their appreciation of the service he had done the province the House of Assembly voted money to defray his funeral expenses, and also to erect a monument to his memory in the Church, which seems never to have been done. In 1782, Baron de Seitz, a Hessian officer, Knight of the Order *pour la Vertu Militaire*, was buried here in full dress, with an orange in his hand, as is the custom when the last baron of a noble German house dies, and shortly after, his fellow-countryman and companion in arms, Baron Kniphausen. In 1784, Lord Charles Greville Montagu, a distinguished officer who had commanded a brave corps of Carolinians in the recent war between Great Britain and Spain, was laid here, and in 1791, with great ceremony, Vice-Admiral John Parr, another royal governor, Bishop Charles Inglis reading the burial service at his funeral. St. Paul's is the resting place of Sir John Wentworth, Bart., who died in 1820, of Chief Justices Jonathan Belcher, Bryan Finucane and Sir Brenton Halliburton, of Bishop Charles Inglis, of the wife of Bishop Stanser, and of other distinguished and titled personages—public officials of Nova Scotia, brave officers of the army and navy, able jurists and statesmen, and noble private citizens, both men and women, who filled well their several spheres in this life and died in the faith of Christ and his Church.

Besides the record for good works St. Paul's has made, there are several facts in her history deserving of especial notice. One of these is of a truly unhappy character. In 1824, the rector, Dr. John Inglis, was raised to the episcopate, and the Crown, having in Dr. Inglis' own case exercised the right of election to the vacant rectorship of St. Paul's, now claimed the same prerogative. This the parishioners would perhaps not have disputed had the appointment of the English authorities been to their mind, but whether by Dr. Inglis' own suggestion or not, it is hard to say, the appointment was given to the Reverend Robert Willis, formerly chaplain of a flag ship, then rector of Trinity Church, St. John, New Brunswick, the parish presenting as their candidate the Reverend John Thomas Twining, for seven years curate of St. Paul's under Dr. Inglis. Mr.

Twining, an earnest man, a decided low church man, and with administrative ability probably quite equal to the demands of the parish, himself felt that he had a prior claim; and so began a heated discussion between the parish and the British Government over the right of presentation, which lasted from October, 1824, until the beginning of 1826, and called out many bitter and acrimonious words. The case seemed so hopeless of peaceful settlement, that it was even put in chancery, but at length the parish was compelled unwillingly to submit and the Reverend Mr. Willis was inducted into the vacant charge. It will be remembered that many of the parishioners of St. Paul's at this time were Loyalists, or the children of Loyalists, proud, highly cultured people with minds of their own, which had not been rendered any more pliable by the experiences they had lately undergone. We are not surprised, therefore, that when they found themselves no longer able to withstand the stronger power, a large number of them left the church. For a time they worshipped as a separate congregation, with Mr., afterward Judge, Johnston as lay reader; but their alienation from the Church only increasing, at length many leading families belonging to the opposition formed an independent congregation which soon allied itself with the already important Baptist denomination and gave it the prestige of their social standing and their wealth. The whole correspondence in this case has been published and forms part of the admirable and painstaking history of the parish prepared for the reports of the Nova Scotia Historical Society by the Reverend Dr. Hill, the fourth rector, himself a representative of one of the best-known Halifax families.

CHAPTER V.

FOUR EARLY MISSIONS.

IN this chapter we must briefly trace the four earliest missions of the Church in Nova Scotia, after that of Halifax: the missions in Lunenburg, Hants and Kings, Annapolis, and Cumberland counties. Nova Scotia is a peninsula, together with the island of Cape Breton, about three hundred and seventy-five miles in extreme length, and about seventy miles in average width, the whole area being twenty thousand eight hundred and eighty-two square miles. The province contains in all eighteen counties and has a population of about four hundred and sixty thousand. Along the Bay of Fundy, from northeast to southwest for about eighty miles, runs the North Mountain, its eastern end terminating in a bold spur or headland at the entrance to Minas Basin, the famous Blomidon,

> "Grim, sullen guardsman
> Of the gate-way of the tide."

and parallel with this the South mountain, between which, with Windsor at its eastern end and Annapolis Royal, the ancient Port Royal, at its western end, lies the fertile Annapolis valley, which includes hundreds of acres of rich alluvial dyke land, formed through long ages by the constant in-flowing of the tide. These dyke lands, which in the whole province comprise perhaps between two and three hundred thousand acres, were in great part reclaimed from the sea by the industrious Acadians, the fruits of whose gigantic toil, people from New England entered into a few years after the forcible removal of the rightful owners of the soil. It is in this fertile valley, some seventy-five miles in length and ten or twelve in width, that the scene of Evangeline is laid, and that much of the most interesting life of Nova Scotia is to be found. Here lie the fine old towns, Windsor, Kentville, Bridgetown and Annapolis, in and around which many a proud family of New England Puritan or New York loyalist descent has lived. In this valley the second and third of the four earliest missions were located, the first, Lunenburg, being on the southwestern shore, the fourth, Cumberland, being farther north toward the isthmus connecting Nova Scotia with New Brunswick.

When the new settlement at Halifax was made, the British government caused proclamations to be issued in the Swiss and German, as well as the English newspapers, offering land to any who would emigrate to the New World. So great were the inducements offered that, as has been already stated, within three or four years from the founding of Halifax, nearly two thousand Germans came to the Province, and these were soon supplemented by a few hundred Swiss and Protestant French. These foreign people were part Calvinists, part Lutherans, and the latter brought with them a schoolmaster who led their worship and gave religious instruction to their children in the Augsburg Confession, to which they loyally held. The little church in Brunswick Street, which they built soon after their arrival, was used both for public worship and for school purposes until March, 1761, when it was consecrated as an Episcopal church, by the Reverend Dr. Breynton, and received the name of St. George's.

In the spring of 1753, it was decided to remove the German settlers from Halifax to Merliguesh, about sixty miles southwestward of Halifax, on the Atlantic sea-board. Block houses, materials and frames for magazines, storehouses, and private dwellings, were got together, and some Boston transports engaged to carry the people and their effects thither. The first settlers arrived early in June, and soon a new town was laid out to which the name of Lunenburg was given. With these settlers, whose number was soon swelled to sixteen hundred, was sent the Reverend Jean Baptiste Moreau, who had been a Roman Catholic priest and prior of the Abbey of St. Matthew, at Brest, but in 1749 had been received into the communion of the Church of England, and at once had been sent out to Halifax as the Society's missionary to the French and Swiss, to whom he first preached, September 9, 1749.

Early in his ministry at Lunenburg, Mr. Moreau, writing to Halifax, says that fifty-six families of Lutherans, Calvinists, Presbyterians, and Anabaptists, had become worthy members of the Church. The mention of the two latter denominations is to be accounted for by the fact that even before the removal of the Germans to Lunenburg, a considerable number of New England fishermen and traders had settled there, some of whom undoubtedly belonged to each of these two religious sects. Mr. Moreau at first held service in the open air, administering the Holy Communion to two hundred at a time under the blue sky.[1] In his mixed parish he ministered in three languages, acting also as missionary to the Indians, several of whose children he baptized. Soon, with the aid of the government, he made preparations for building a church, for the frame of which, as of St. Paul's, an order was sent to Boston, in the remote colony of Massachusetts Bay. Soon he writes the Society that there are more than two hundred regular communicants of French and Germans, who are entirely reconciled to the Church of England, and in a letter dated October 1, 1755, he says that his French congregation increases every day, that they attend divine service regularly, and that there are seldom less than eighty or ninety communicants. In the preceding six months

---
[1] Desbrisay's "History of Lunenburg."

he had baptized thirty-nine children, married sixteen couples, and buried three grown persons and a few children. The Society's schoolmaster, working under his direction, was named Bailly. The same year the Reverend Thomas Wood, in his summer itinerancy, came to Lunenburg and performed the service in English, and with the assistance of Mr. Moreau, administered the Holy Communion to twenty-four Germans. At that time, it is said, in addition to the regular inhabitants, there were about a hundred and twenty English soldiers in the garrison at Lunenburg. Mr. Moreau's work there continued until early in 1770, when he died. His son, Cornwallis Moreau, was the first male child born in Halifax, and was named in the Lunenburg grant.

In 1761, the Society appointed Reverend Joseph Bennett itinerant missionary in Nova Scotia, with instructions to officiate chiefly at Lunenburg, "but occasionally also, as need shall require, in the several other townships which are or shall be erected in the Province, as the Governor shall direct, till the bounds of his mission are more fully settled." The new missionary was in the thirty-fourth year of his

age, and was recommended to the Society as a
man of good temper, prudence and learning,
and of a sober and pious conversation, zealous
for the Christian religion, thoroughly well affected to the government, and one who had
always conformed to the doctrine and discipline of the Church of England. Mr. Bennett
was, therefore, born probably in 1728, and came
from England to Nova Scotia in 1762. His
appointment to Lunenburg was made by the
S. P. G., but the lieutenant-governor of Nova
Scotia, Jonathan Belcher, feeling the pressing
need of an English missionary and choolmaster at Lunenburg, and not knowing of the
Society's appointment, had engaged the Reverend Robert Vincent for this double service.
Accordingly, on petition of Mr. Belcher, the
Society cancelled its own appointment, and
ratified the lieutenant-governor's choice, sending Mr. Bennett instead to Horton, Falmouth,
Newport, and Cornwallis, with a salary of
seventy pounds sterling for each place. In
council, August 7, 1761, it was advised, that
the Reverend Robert Vincent be appointed to
minister at Lunenburg, at a salary of seventy
pounds, and twenty pounds per annum as

schoolmaster. August 13th, it was advised "that the Reverend Mr. Robert Vincent be admitted to celebrate Divine service in the Church at Lunenburg, and there perform all rites and ceremonies according to the usages of the Church of England, alternately with the Reverend Mr. Moreau; and that Colonel Sutherland be requested, accordingly, to adjust all matters relating to the Church between Mr. Moreau and Mr. Vincent." It is stated that Mr. Vincent was "remarkable for zealous application and moderate conduct in the course of his mission," and that in faithfulness to duty he went even beyond his strength. He died in 1766.[1]

Two other early clergymen at Lunenburg were the Reverend Paulus Bryzelius, who had formerly been a Lutheran minister, and the Reverend Peter de la Roche. Mr. Bryzelius, before coming to Nova Scotia, had been ordained by the Bishop of London for the German mission at Lunenburg. He was for a time contemporary with Mr. Moreau, his work, especially among the young, being warmly eulogized by Lieutenant-Governor Francklin

---

[1] Murdoch's "History of Nova Scotia," Vol. II., p. 406.

and Chief Justice Belcher. He is said to have held three services every Sunday, one in English, one in French, and one in German. For his use, the English authorities sent out a large number of German Prayer Books, and he himself translated a catechism. At Easter, 1768, forty-six young persons were brought by him to the Holy Communion, and in September, 1769, he reported the number of children in his mission under twelve years of age, as six hundred and eighty-four, of which number he himself had baptized a hundred and twenty-nine. At Easter, 1770, he admitted to the Holy Communion thirty persons, making the total number of communicants in the Lunenburg mission, English, French, and German, two hundred and one. Mr. Bryzelius was struck with apoplexy, while preaching, on Good Friday, 1773, and died in half an hour. He was buried exactly under the pulpit of the church in which he died. He was sixty years old.

The Reverend Peter de la Roche, a native of Geneva, was ordained to the cure of Lunenburg in 1771. About this time Reverend Mr. Muhlenburg, president of the Lutheran Synod in Philadelphia, was applied to by Calvinists and Lutherans for a missionary. He advised both to adhere to the English Church and for this advice was thanked by the Halifax committee, who requested "that no declaration, or measure should at any time be used to disturb or prevent Calvinists and Lutherans in the full exercise of their religious principles and mode of divine worship." In 1773, through the agency of Mr. de la Roche, a school-house was built for the French at Lunenburg. Mr. de la Roche also studied German, and by 1775, was able to officiate in the three languages. During the American war, his salary being very small, he suffered for provisions. While he lived in Lunenburg, he published several excellent sermons and a commentary on the four gospels. One of these sermons was entitled "The Gospel of Christ, Preached to the Poor, Repent ye, etc. St. Peter, in Acts iii. 19; printed at the author's expense, to be given, and not to be sold. 'Freely ye have received, freely give.' Jesus Christ, in Matt. x. 28." Francklin Bulkeley Gould, son of Reverend Peter de la Roche and Ann his wife, was baptized May 27, 1773. In the entry of this baptism, the fact is noticed, that this was the first child in the province inoculated for small-pox.

In 1776, Mr. de la Roche writes that he has over a hundred and ten communicants, that during the year he has baptized twenty-eight children, married five couples, and buried twenty persons, the greater part of them infants under a year, twelve of whom have died of small-pox. He writes that he celebrates the Lord's Supper seven times a year, three times in English, at the Great Festivals, twice in German, and twice in French. In 1778, he writes that he has been employed in repairing his church, which was ready to fall to the ground. In this he has been assisted by the lieutenant-governor, who, himself, has contributed fifty pounds. In 1780, he reports, that of the three nationalities included in his mission, there are about thirty families of French, and a hundred of Germans, while the English are chiefly people from New England, very few being from England or Ireland.

The Reverend Joseph Bennett, who was at first sent to the Lunenburg mission, was soon transferred to the interior of the province. His field of labor was the portion of country now comprised in the two counties, Hants and Kings, the latter of which embraces the chief part of what, from its great agricultural richness, has long been known as the "Garden of Nova Scotia." In 1750, the province was divided into five counties—Annapolis, Kings, Cumberland, Lunenburg, and Halifax. Later these were subdivided, so that there are now, as has been said, fourteen counties in Nova Scotia proper, besides the four which the island of Cape Breton comprises. The two townships of Newport and Falmouth, which were part of Mr. Bennett's mission, are now in Hants county; then, like Cornwallis and Horton, to the inhabitants of which he also ministered, they were in King's. It is this latter county that is chiefly known as "the Land of Evangeline." Here on the shores of Mines Basin, in Acadian times:

"Distant, secluded still, the little village of Grand Pré
   Lay in the fruitful valley. Vast meadows stretched to
      the eastward,
   Giving the village its name, and pasture to flocks
      without number.
   Dikes that the hands of the farmers had raised with
      labor incessant,
   Shut out the turbulent tides; but at stated seasons
      the flood gates

Four Early Missions. 79

Opened, and welcomed the sea to wander at will o'er
  the meadows.
West and south there were fields of flax, and orchards
  and cornfields
Spreading afar and unfenced o'er the plain; and
  away to the northward
Blomidon rose, and the forests old, and aloft on the
  mountains
Sea fogs pitched their tents, and mists from the
  mighty Atlantic
Looked on the happy valley but ne'er from their
  station descended.
There, in the midst of its farms, reposed the Acadian
  village."

From this beautiful region, as well as from what are now Hants, Cumberland, and Annapolis counties, the Acadians, to the number of perhaps six thousand, were expelled with the sanction of the British Government, in 1755; and in 1760–62, in response to a proclamation offering their lands to New England settlers, many intelligent people, chiefly from Connecticut, Massachusetts, and Rhode Island, took up their residence in the depopulated districts. These new settlers were in many cases people of good family and of means, but they were, almost without exception, Congregationalists, whose ancestors for four generations had been alienated from the Church of England, and who themselves had little sympathy with the Church's worship. It was to these New Englanders, among whom there was no doubt, at least about Fort Edward, a sprinkling of English-born people, that Mr. Bennett was sent by the Society in 1762. In 1763, through Jonathan Belcher, Esq., then President of the Council, Mr. Bennett proposed to the Society the establishment of two schoolmasters, one in Horton and Cornwallis, the other in Falmouth and Newport. He reported that the inhabitants of Cornwallis proposed to build a church, that at Horton a subscription was already opened for purchasing a house to hold service in, and that the people were inclined to make some provision for a schoolmaster, who, with their subscriptions and the Society's allowance, together with a lot of land set apart in every township for a schoolmaster, might live very comfortably. Mr. Bennett's own letter to the Society, dated January 4, 1763, states that he has now been settled in Kings County six weeks, and that he finds in Horton six hundred and seventy persons, of whom three hundred and seventy-five are children, in Cornwallis five hundred and eighteen, of whom three hundred and nineteen are children, in Falmouth two hundred and seventy-eight, of whom a hundred and forty-six are children, and in Newport two hundred and fifty-one, of whom a hundred and eleven are children. In another letter, dated July of the same year, Mr. Bennett writes that his success in his mission has far exceeded his expectation; that he has baptized sixteen, buried three, and married three couples, and that he has in all eighteen communicants. September 18, 1764, he states that he now officiates at five places, "the Governor having ordered him to take Fort Edward in rotation, on account of a difficult and dangerous river, which renders it impossible, at least five months in the year, for the inhabitants near that fort to attend Divine Worship at the place appointed." To perform the regular duties of his mission on Sundays, he had, at this time, to ride nearly two hundred miles a month. In the preceding half-year he had baptized fifty-two children and one adult, and he reports that as the prejudices of the people against the Church wear off, the duties of his ministry greatly increase. During Mr. Bennett's incumbency of this mission, in 1771, a chapel was built by subscription at Windsor, which seems to have been used for other services than those of the Church, and for school purposes as well. It stood on the northwest corner of the old burying ground, on an inclosed plot sixty feet square. In 1772, or '73, a church was built at Cornwallis by Messrs. John Burbidge and William Best, which was not finished, however, until 1776; and November 10, 1783, the Assembly voted a hundred pounds for a church at Falmouth.

In 1774, the Reverend William Ellis was appointed by the Society an itinerant missionary to Nova Scotia, and reached the province, late in the same year, after a long and tedious voyage, and some delays on the New England coast. Arriving here, he and Mr. Bennett made an exchange, whereby Mr. Ellis was to take part of Mr. Bennett's mission, and the latter was to devote himself in great part to itinerant labor. This exchange did not please the Society, who assented to it only on condition that Mr. Ellis should take the whole of Mr. Bennett's mission, and that Mr. Bennett should give himself exclusively to itinerant work. The matter being thus settled, Mr. Bennett

entered upon his wider field, and the only
place with which his name is henceforth connected in the Society's reports is Cape Sable
on the southwestern shore. In the report for
1780, it is stated that the Society have received
the sad intelligence that the Reverend Mr.
Bennett is confined at Windsor, greatly dis-
ordered both in body and mind, so that the
physicians are of opinion that he will never
again be serviceable. This is the last mention
of him in the Society's reports, and it seems
probable that he died soon after, and was
buried at Windsor.

In 1776, Mr. Ellis writes to the Society rather
discouragedly regarding his mission, the lack
of church buildings especially seeming to give
him much concern. He has no church at Newport, he says, though his congregation is largest
there. At Falmouth he is trying to get an old
building repaired for worship; at Windsor the
building used as a church is "applied to various purposes, and occasionally to very im-
proper ones." To this latter, Governor Legge
has made a present of some handsome church
furniture, but the building is unfit to receive
it. He reports, however, in his whole mission

ninety communicants. In 1779, he writes more hopefully. At Windsor, where he resides, he says he has "a very regular little flock and takes much pleasure in them." In Cornwallis there are upwards of a thousand inhabitants, "most of them well affected to the Church, and very desirous of having a minister to themselves," while in Falmouth and Newport together, there are about the same number of inhabitants, many of whom attend service regularly, and behave well. In the previous year he has baptized fifty-six persons, buried nine, and married sixteen couples. In his mission he has now seventy-nine communicants. In 1782, he writes that the people of Falmouth have come to the determination to erect a church and he hopes their example will be followed by his Newport parishioners. In the same year his large mission was divided, Cornwallis and Horton, with Wilmot added, forming one mission, to which the Reverend John Wiswell, formerly at Falmouth, Maine, was appointed, the stations in Hants county remaining under his own charge. In this smaller mission Mr. Ellis labored until 1795, when he died, and was buried in the Windsor churchyard. His tombstone there bears the following inscription:

> "Here lies the body of the REV. WILLIAM ELLIS,
> who departed this life, the 5th of June, 1795,
> in the 65th year of his age.
> He was rector of the church of Windsor
> 21 years."

The New England settlers on the lands of the exiled Acadians were not limited to the country about Minas Basin, but were found also in considerable numbers in the western part of the province. In June, 1760, at Port Rossignol, now Liverpool, they already numbered seventy heads of families, while at Annapolis, and several other places along the southwestern coast, there were perhaps quite as many. At Annapolis there were of this and other classes, enough Church people to make a mission necessary and to give a Church clergyman foothold, once more. In 1753, as we learn from the report of the S. P. G. of the following year, the Reverend Thomas Wood had spent some time at Annapolis where, in the words of the certificate of the chief officers of the garrison, "he had performed with great diligence all the duties of his function there, and behaved himself well in every respect."

Mr. Wood was probably a native of New Jersey, for in 1749, on petition of the inhabitants of New Brunswick, in that state, who declare him to be "a gentleman of a very good life and conversation, bred to Physick and Surgery," having gone to England for the purpose, he was ordained deacon and priest by the Bishop of London, and sent home to take charge of the churches of New Brunswick and Elizabeth Town. While he retained this cure he lived at New Brunswick and officiated at Elizabeth Town twice a month, but he soon left New Jersey for Nova Scotia, where, after his visit to Annapolis, he labored until 1764, either as an itinerant missionary, or as assistant to Dr. Breynton in Halifax.

In 1761, the Reverend Dr. Breynton of St. Paul's made three visits to the "new settlements" in Hants and Kings counties, and proceeded as far as Annapolis, for which extra labor the Society ordered him a gratuity. In 1762, Mr. Wood, who was assisting Dr. Breynton, went twice over the same ground, and in 1763 twice more, finding at Granville and Annapolis, as he writes the Society, more than eight hundred souls without either church or minister. In this year the Society requested Mr. Wood to undertake once more the charge of Annapolis, and when they knew that he had consented to do so, the people, he says, were full of joy at the prospect of having him again among them. At his last visit in 1763 he promised to be with them the next spring and in the mean time he engaged Mr. James Wilkie as lay reader and schoolmaster. In 1764, he entered on his charge and almost immediately began the study of Micmac, so that he might minister to the Indians in this part of the province, and accomplish his purpose of translating the Book of Common Prayer into the Micmac tongue. Sprague's "Annals of the American Pulpit," says: Mr. Wood "applied himself to a study of the Micmac language with no other assistance than he could derive from the papers of M. Maillard, and fully determined to persevere until he should be able to publish a grammar, a dictionary, and a translation of the Bible. In 1766, he sent home the first volume of his grammar with a translation of the Creed, the Lord's Prayer, etc., and was now able to minister to the Indians in their own language. In 1769, by re-

quest of the governor, he made a missionary tour among the settlements on the St. John River, New Brunswick, and was received by the Indians with every expression of respect."[*]
Of the progress of Mr. Wood's work among the Micmacs, he himself writes in 1767, that he is now able to read prayers to the Indians in their own language. This he had done the previous July at St. Paul's, in Halifax, in presence of Lord William Campbell, the governor-in-chief, Colonel Dalrymple, and most of the officers of the army and navy, and the inhabitants. On this occasion, as was described in the last chapter, the Indians sang an anthem before and after service, and before service began an Indian chief came forward from the rest, and kneeling down prayed that Almighty God would bless His Majesty, King George III., their lawful king and governor, and that prosperity might rest upon His Majesty's province of Nova Scotia. He then rose up and Mr. Wood at his desire explained his prayer in English to the whole congregation. Upon this, says the S. P. G. report, His Excellency turned and bowed to all the Indians. When

---

[*] Sprague's "Annals," vol. v., p. 328.

service was ended the Indians thanked God, the Governor, and Mr. Wood, for the opportunity they had had of hearing prayers in their own language. All this reminds one a little of modern denominational Sunday-school doings, and it may well be questioned how much real feeling it indicated on the part of the Micmacs, but it certainly argues a deep interest in his work on Mr. Wood's part, and shows that personally he had gained some influence over these simple-minded savages. On the 12th of August, 1767, it is further stated in the report, Mr. Wood married Pierre Jaques, an Indian, to Marie Joseph, eldest daughter of old King Thoma, who regarded himself as hereditary king of the Micmacs, the persons present at the wedding, besides the Indians, being Sir Thomas Rich, an English baronet, and several other gentlemen. Soon after the ceremony, we also learn, the clergyman entertained the Indians at his own house.

At Annapolis Mr. Wood labored faithfully, and with much success until his death which occurred there, December 14, 1778. His wife died some time in the same year. He was succeeded by the Reverend Joshua Wingate

Weeks, one of the Loyalist clergymen who had lately taken refuge in the province from the revolting colonies.

The Annapolis Royal mission does not seem to have grown very rapidly, for in 1774 Mr. Wood writes that his communicants number only from twenty to thirty. He seems, however, not to have been unpopular with the Independents there, for he says that the greatest part of the Dissenters "occasionally attend him on Sundays." At what time S. P. G. churches were built at Annapolis and Granville, the Society's records do not show, but in 1775, it is said, so many new settlers had come that the churches could not hold the congregations. The Annapolis people therefore in that year "with great cheerfulness," subscribed one hundred and sixty pounds toward the building of a church, which should be sixty feet long by forty feet wide. A church was, likewise, begun at Granville; but in 1783, the Annapolis church, although inclosed and glazed, was still unfinished, although it was expected that it would soon be made ready for service. The school at this time was taught by Mr. Benjamin Snow, who had been educated at Dartmouth College. In 1783, fifty-two Church families are reported at Annapolis, and in 1784, over twenty communicants there, and between thirty and forty at Granville.

The fourth mission in Nova Scotia, after Halifax, was established in Cumberland county, in 1768. This county lies northeast of the Bay of Fundy on the border of New Brunswick, and contains the site of the historic Fort Cumberland, better known by its musical French name, *Beau Séjour*. Many of the inhabitants of this part of Nova Scotia were North of Ireland Presbyterians, who had first emigrated to New Hampshire, but after a few years had removed to Nova Scotia; some were New England people who had entered into possession of the French farms and dykes in that part of the Acadian land. The first missionary sent to Cumberland was the Reverend J. Eagleson, who had been a clergyman of the Established Church of Scotland, and for some time had been laboring in Nova Scotia, but in 1768 received ordination from the Bishop of London, being strongly recommended to his lordship by Mr. Francklin, the lieutenant-governor, Mr. Belcher, the chief-justice, Mr. Bulkeley, the provincial secretary, and the Reverend Dr. Breynton, who states that Mr. Eagleson had left his former ministry from real conviction. June 27, 1768, Mr. Eagleson arrived from England, ordained, but instead of being sent at once to his appointed mission, the lieutenant-governor directed him to "repair during pleasure" to the island of St. John. After some little time spent in that island he went, however, to Cumberland, and in 1773, he reports to the Society, that since the departure of Mr. Gannett, the Dissenting minister, his congregation has gradually increased, the number of Dissenters who regularly attend the public service being nearly equal to his own people; that seventeen English families have settled in that and the adjacent townships, and many more are expected; and that he has found a schoolmaster for his mission if the Society will appoint him. In 1774 it is reported that Mr. Eagleson preaches also "to a full and decent congregation at Sackville or Trantamore, as often as the roads and the season will permit;" and that in the last year he has baptized thirty-seven children, married six couples, and buried three persons. During the summer of 1774, this clergyman visited the townships of Hillsborough and Monckton on the river Peticodiac, in New Brunswick, holding service among the English and Dutch settlers there and baptizing fourteen children. In Cumberland and the adjacent townships of Fort Lawrence, Amherst, and Sackville he baptized within a short time seventeen children, married nine couples, buried one child, and gathered sixteen communicants.

During the Revolutionary war, the Cumberland people, almost alone of the inhabitants of Nova Scotia, showed great sympathy with the Whigs of the older colonies. Indeed their temper and their movements were such as to create considerable alarm in the minds of the Nova Scotia authorities, who soon found it necessary to send a large force to keep them in check. For a time it was rumored that Nova Scotia was to be invaded by people from New England; and in fact, Fort Cumberland, in 1776, was seized by about five hundred people from Machias, Maine, under the direction of four of the prominent Cumberland rebels. At the time of this disturbance a few private persons were molested, among them Mr. Eagleson, who was taken prisoner and carried to

Massachusetts Bay, where he remained in prison for sixteen months, at last escaping, and returning home to find his property completely destroyed. He then asked and obtained of the Society leave to go to England "to see an aged parent," his mission, however, to be supplied in his absence. It is said that during the Revolution, two hundred persons in Cumberland rose against the government, and that the people of Truro, Onslow, and Londonderry, with the exception of five persons, refused to take the oath of allegiance. The punishment proposed by the government for these rebels certainly sounds unique; it was determined to treat them as Popish recusants.

CHAPTER VI.

THE COMING OF THE LOYALISTS.

OUR rapid survey of the five earliest missions of the Church in Nova Scotia has brought us to the period of the war of the Revolution in the older American colonies. We have seen the missionaries of the S. P. G. at work among the English and New England people of Halifax, the Germans and Swiss of Lunenburg, the New England settlers in Hants, Kings, and Annapolis counties, the Indians about the old Port Royal garrison, and the Scotch-Irish and New England inhabitants of Cumberland county, the most northerly district in Nova Scotia then reached by the Church. With the war of the Revolution an entirely new element came into Nova Scotia. There were many in the revolting colonies who could not sympathize with the prevailing bitterness against the mother country, and who either absolutely refused to take any part in the disturbance, or else speedily joined the British side. Among these United Empire Loyalists were many of the foremost men of the leading colonies, especially New York and Massachusetts, who, as the strife grew fiercer, and the fury of the violent Whigs increased, found themselves proscribed and banished, their property confiscated, and in some cases even their lives endangered. In this state of things a movement toward settlement in Nova Scotia was begun, and by 1784, between thirty-five and forty thousand Loyalists, it is estimated, had found refuge in the province of Nova Scotia, which then had its boundary at the river St. Croix.[1]

The emigration of Loyalists to Nova Scotia began at the evacuation of Boston in 1776, when more than fourteen hundred of the inhabitants of Massachusetts went with the British troops to Halifax. In September, 1782, three hundred from New York, landed at Annapolis, the next being five hundred unfortunate Carolinians, who fled from Charleston at its evacuation. In January, 1783, the governor

---

[1] Hannay puts the number as high as this; it has commonly been put at not more than thirty thousand. Hannay thinks that a hundred thousand, in all, went to Nova Scotia, Upper and Lower Canada, England, and the West India Islands.

notified Sir Thomas Johnston, the minister in England, of future arrivals, but it was not until April of that year that the chief emigration began. Then, a fleet of twenty vessels left New York for the river St. John, having on board three thousand Loyalists, men, women, and children. June 6, 1783, Governor Parr informs Lord North, the secretary of state, that since January 15th, upwards of seven thousand refugees have arrived in Nova Scotia, these, he says, to be followed by three thousand of the provincial forces, and others besides. July 6th, he writes that a considerable number of Loyalists at New York desire to make a settlement in Cape Breton Island, and September 30th, he writes that from November last to the end of July, upwards of thirteen thousand persons have arrived at Annapolis, Halifax, Port Roseway (Shelburne), St. John River, and Cumberland, and that numbers have since landed, so that there are now probably eighteen thousand in the province. At Shelburne, he says, there are about five thousand, and many others are expected. He does not know how many may still come to the province, but he is informed by Sir Guy Carleton that eight or ten thousand will probably "be forced by the violent temper of the American committees to seek an asylum here." About this time two thousand more Loyalists did come, in addition to the eight thousand Shelburne settlers, who sailed from New York, Long Island, and Staten Island in the famous September fleet. In the next two months several ship loads more came, so that in November the governor estimated the whole number in the province as over twenty-five thousand.

With the coming of the Loyalists, Halifax developed into a prosperous and busy city with signs of wealth and culture everywhere. To accommodate the thousands that came to the western and southern shores, new settlements were made—Shelburne, Digby, Weymouth; and in other parts of the province, Wilmot, and Guysborough, besides the numerous settlements in the newly-constituted province of New Brunswick. While most of the older communities had their populations thus reinforced, the inhabitants of Nova Scotia were at this time still further increased by many negroes from the plantations in the South who had escaped to freedom. To settle all these new people in homes, properly to apportion lands for their use, and at the same time to keep in check the rebellious spirit of the inhabitants of Cumberland, required the most vigilant care of the provincial authorities.

Nor did the Loyalists start for Nova Scotia without sufficient guaranty on the part of the British Government itself. Sir Guy Carleton seems to have been empowered to make any arrangement for their welfare that seemed best to him, and near the close of the Revolution, being waited on at New York by the Reverend Dr. Seabury, then of Westchester, and Colonel Benjamin Thompson, of the King's American Dragoons, gave distinct assurance that the Loyalists intending to go to Nova Scotia should be provided with vessels to carry them and their belongings, with provisions for the voyage; and for those who needed such assistance food and clothing for a year after landing, or else money to purchase, besides building materials and fire-arms. More important than all, it was promised that convenient tracts of from three to six hundred acres of land should be set off for each family, and in every township, land should be granted for a church and a school. Nothwithstanding these liberal provisions for their welfare, the Loyalists, wrenched from homes of comfort, and in many cases of luxury, with life-long, tender, human ties rudely snapped, compelled to begin life anew under strange, hard conditions, must have suffered deeply.

The relation borne by this story of the Loyalist emigration to the history of the Church in Nova Scotia, is of course clear. The Loyalists were, almost without exception, Church people, who in the new communities where they now found themselves, aimed to establish the ancient worship according to the Book of Common Prayer.

No class fared more hardly in the Revolution than the Episcopal clergy. That they were the upholders on this continent of an institution that in England was part and parcel of the state, was of itself sufficient to make them the objects of suspicion, but it was also true that in the beginning of the conflict they almost without exception openly espoused the British side. It would be surprising indeed if they had done otherwise, since not only were they all the agents of an English society, from which they drew their pay, but in ordination had vowed to be loyal to the English sovereign. There were some few clergymen in the revolting colonies who were able to interpret this promise as a vow of loyalty to whoever might be in authority—a general promise to do what lay in their power to uphold good government—but the majority were not able thus to settle the matter with their consciences, and there is no doubt that in most instances their sympathies as well as their convictions were all in favor of yielding to whatever laws the mother country might see fit to make. In most cases they held on to their parishes as long as they were permitted, or found it at all safe to do so; then many of them fled within the British lines or secretly took themselves off to England or to some of the still loyal colonies. In the brief biographies of Loyalist clergymen, in a later chapter, it will be seen how large a number were driven from their old homes to Nova Scotia or New Brunswick;[1] while the new missions start-

---

[1] At the beginning of the War of Independence there were in all the American colonies, from Maine to Georgia, less than three hundred parishes, and not far from two hundred and fifty clergymen.

ed in these provinces under their auspices will attest their continued zeal for the Church, of which they were ministers, and the Church's worship. Their sufferings were in many cases most severe. They were mobbed, whipped, shot at, imprisoned, fined, and banished; their property was confiscated or wantonly destroyed, their services were disturbed, their altars defiled, their churches wrecked, and their writings burned. Some of them died of poverty and exposure. Reverend Dr. Caner writes the Society from Halifax that he and several other clergymen had been obliged to leave Boston at a moment's warning, with the loss of all their property. Reverend Dr. Byles came to Halifax with five motherless children, and for a time was deprived of all means of support. Reverend Jacob Bailey reports that for three years past he has undergone the most severe and cruel treatment. In May, 1776, he was seized by the committee and after being treated with the utmost abuse, was laid under heavy bonds for refusing to read a proclamation for a general fast, and a few months after was summoned before the same committee for not publishing the Declaration of Independence, after which he was declared an enemy to his country and ordered to appear before the general court, at a distance of a hundred and eighty miles, in the midst of winter. Visiting a settlement, about fifty miles from his home, to preach and baptize, he was assaulted by a violent armed mob, who stripped him naked in search of papers, pretending that he had formed a design of escaping to Quebec. Being afterwards cleared on a trial of transportation, in a full town meeting, the magistrates were so incensed that they issued a warrant to apprehend him, which induced him to remain a close prisoner in his house for many weeks, to the great detriment of his health. At length he fled in the night, through fear of an armed mob ready to seize him, and wandered about the provinces of Maine, New Hampshire, and Massachusetts, till the act expired, after which for three months he was violently persecuted by the high sheriff for not taking the oath of abjuration. Then he obtained leave to depart from Maine, but was prevented by the severity of the weather and other circumstances, for six months, during which time he was violently persecuted by the sheriff who declared that he should either abjure the king or be sent to prison, both of which, however, through his constant vigilance and the kindness of his parishioners, he was able to avoid. In short, he was twice mobbed, four times sentenced to heavy bonds and hurried from one tribunal to another, three times driven from his family and obliged to roam about the country disguised, his family meanwhile suffering and he himself sometimes going without food for twenty-four hours at a time. He was twice fired at, his servant was imprisoned in his absence, and when at last he and his family were able to escape to Halifax, they were destitute of money, had nothing left of their property but two old feather beds, and had hardly enough clothing to cover them. Reverend John Sayre writes that he had lost his all—that he had not even a change of clothing for himself or his family, and that he had been obliged to borrow money to enable him to remove to Nova Scotia. Reverend Isaac Browne, an old clergyman, between forty and fifty years a missionary in New Jersey, is reported as having reached Annapolis, penniless, after a month's "tedious and tempestuous" voyage, which had so affected his wife as to bring on delirium from which there was little hope of her recovering. These were a few of the many cases of suffering among its missionaries, reported at this time to the S. P. G., which in conjunction with the governments of Nova Scotia, and the newly-formed province of New Brunswick, and with the kindly aid of the rector of St. Paul's in Halifax, did all it could to alleviate their distress.

The unsettled period of the Revolution was thus the real beginning of the Church in Nova Scotia. During the whole of it the few older missionaries in the province were most active in their missions, but in succeeding chapters it will be shown how many new churches, under these exiled Loyalist clergymen, were now actively started. Notwithstanding the number of clergymen who came from the older colonies, the needs of the greatly-increased population were not soon met, and the constant appeals for more missionaries, especially in the peninsula of Nova Scotia, are truly pathetic. From Cornwallis, Mr. Wiswell, and from Annapolis, Mr. Bailey, annually report themselves as having made long and tedious journeys to minister to people in the new settlements, who have neither church nor minister, and who greatly desire both. In 1784, Mr. Bailey writes that he has visited Digby, a newly-settled town, about twenty miles from Annapolis, where he has held service. He speaks with approbation of Mr. Forman, "a refugee and half-pay officer, who was the principal schoolmaster there, and who, observing the growing evils in that populous settlement, arising from the want of public worship and from the abuse and profanation of the Lord's day, had accustomed himself to assemble his pupils in particular on that day, and to read the Church service and a sermon to them;" the result of which was soon crowded audiences, and a visible alteration in the manners of the people. Other large settlements and towns, he writes, are daily forming, "where scarcely a vestige of human cultivation and resort existed before the late calamitous emigration." "These unfortunate exiles," he says, "wish the Society to know how anxious they are for the ministrations of religion, and since, deprived of their property as they have been, and obliged to begin the world anew, it will be some years before they are able to support ministers, they implore the assistance of their charitable brethren in Europe." Digby, especially, Mr. Bailey recommends to the notice of the Society. The town is compact and contains five hundred families of loyal refugees, and he thinks there is no part of the province where a minister could be of more service.

In the peninsula of Nova Scotia, between 1784, and 1790, we find the following appointments made by the S. P. G. To Digby, Reverend Roger Viets, to Shelburne, Reverend William Walter and Reverend John Rowland, to Parrsborough, Reverend Thomas Shreve, to Wilmot, Reverend John Wiswell, to Guysborough, Reverend Peter de la Roche, to Yarmouth,.Reverend George Panton, and to Granville, Reverend Archibald Peane Inglis, who is said to have been a nephew of Bishop Charles Inglis. The reports from these new missions at the close of the century, show activity and growth. Granville has been set off from Annapolis Royal, because "the rapid river" that runs between these two places, makes frequent services there impossible, and because there is a numerous population who desire a settled clergyman, the Dissenters being willing to turn their meeting house over to the Church. Aylesford and Wilmot are too far removed from Cornwallis and Horton to be longer joined with them, and so the bishop and Mr. James Morden together have given four hundred acres of land in Aylesford for a glebe, and a church has been begun at Wilmot, and a clergyman settled there. The missionary at Annapolis Royal has added part of the new Loyalist settlement of Clements, containing sixty families, to his already large field, the Reverend Mr. Viets of Digby having taken the other part. The Digby mission has somewhat suffered by the return to the United States of sixty families, but a church is building and the mission has, on the whole, so prospered that Mr. Viets has now twenty-seven white, and seventeen black communicants. At Parrsborough a church is nearly done, and its missionary, the Reverend Mr. Shreve, reports thirteen communicants.

CHAPTER VII.
THE FIRST COLONIAL BISHOP.

IN his admirable history of the American Episcopal Church, Dr. McConnell has recorded the successive plans made by the bishops in England, and the successive appeals made by Churchmen in the colonies for the complete equipment of the Church in the new world. Early in the 17th century Archbishop Laud had a scheme to send out a bishop to keep the Puritans in check in America, as he himself was trying to do in England; later, Tenison and Compton, Bishops of London, and Secker, Archbishop of Canterbury, vainly labored for the same end. On this side the water many plans for the Episcopate were made. In 1695, at the time of the capture of New York, the Reverend Mr. Miller, chaplain of the fort, proposed that the Bishop of London should consecrate a suffragan for New York, the province being a Crown colony. His plan was to take the king's farm for a bishop's seat, and build a bishop's church, the large sums of money raised in England for missions in America to be administered, and in short, general jurisdiction over the missions on the whole American continent to be had by the bishop who should be appointed. Chaplain Miller's excellent plan failed, but in 1702, Messrs. Keith and Talbot, the first missionaries of the S. P. G., again urged strongly America's need of the Episcopate. "I don't doubt," writes Talbot, "that some good man with one hundred pounds a year would do the Church more service than with a coach and six a hundred years hence." A little later he writes his friend, Mr. Keith, that several of the clergy, both of New York and Maryland, have said that they would pay their tenths to a bishop—the man then proposed being a Mr. John Lillingston—as the vice-gerent of my Lord of London, "whereby the Bishop of America might have as honorable provision as some in Europe." In a letter to the S. P. G. he writes rather sharply of the little attention paid in England to the call that, like Macedonia, America had so long been sending across the sea. In 1705, a convocation of fourteen clergymen at Burlington sent a petition to the Archbishop of London, representing that many Lutheran and Independent ministers were ready to conform to the Church if a bishop were here to ordain them. In 1709, the officers of the Venerable Society, possibly at the instigation of, certainly seconded by their trusted Francis Nicholson, then Governor of Maryland, begged Queen Anne "that a colonial bishopric might be endowed out of the proceeds of the lands ceded by the Council of Utrecht; but the death of the queen put an end to the project." In 1715, the Society again took the matter up, proposing to George I. that four bishops should be consecrated, one for Barbadoes, one for Jamaica, one to have his seat at Burlington, New Jersey, and one at Williamsburg, Virginia; but the Scottish rebellion breaking out, this appeal, like the others, went unanswered, and no new scheme was proposed until fifty years more had gone by. In 1765, a new petition came from the American colonies themselves. This time the clergy of Pennsylvania, New Jersey, and New York all united in an appeal to the authorities at home. But still the Church refused to act. A few bishops and agents of the S. P. G. were fairly well informed regarding the plantations and felt some responsibility concerning their spiritual needs, but to English Churchmen at large the colonies were too far away much to stir their imaginations, too mythical to move their hearts to missionary zeal. By-and-by, when the Episcopate became a greater possibility, the colonies had begun to think of separating from the mother country, or at least had begun strongly to desire home rule, and a suspicion was abroad that the appointment of bishops would serve rather to strengthen than weaken the authority of the Crown. As the Revolution approached, the prospect, of course, grew darker, until the land was plunged in war, and the Church, in the minds of the majority, the friend of a hostile power, seemed on the point of losing forever her influence, if not her identity in the western world.

When the war closed it was plain that something must be done, for the Church was now left "without reputation, without money, without men." In the process of reorganization and readjustment it was most natural that Churchmen should more than ever desire the Episcopate, for it was now clearer than it had ever been that the Church in America must be fully equipped if she was to live and grow. Accordingly in Connecticut, where "the controlling motive was ecclesiastical," and where "the Church idea had been far better wrought out" than elsewhere, and where, indeed, the strength of the Church in New England chiefly lay, on the 25th of March, 1783, a company of clergymen met secretly at Woodbury, a little village among the hills of Litchfield county, and chose for the Episcopate, which they were determined now to secure, the Reverend Dr. Jeremiah Leaming and the Reverend Dr. Samuel Seabury, both Connecticut men by birth, though now in New York, one or the other of whom they hoped might be prevailed upon to accept the high office, even with the dangers and difficulties which they clearly enough foresaw would attend it. They were not even certain that whoever might be consecrated would be permitted to live in the United States, but they said: "If he is not, then we can establish him across the border, in Nova Scotia, and send our candidates for ordination to him there until better times shall dawn." Dr. Leaming was an old man and declined the office; he could not face the dangers and discomforts of the long sea voyages to and from England, nor had he strength for the labor and care that must fall on the first American bishop in such troublous times. But Dr. Seabury, who was younger, accepted, and a little more than two months later, in Admiral Digby's returning flag ship, sailed to England, where he vainly tried for a year to get consecration. At last, finding that farther attempts in England would be useless, he went north to Scotland, and by the bishops of the "obscure and broken" non juring Scottish Episcopal Church, Robert Kilgour, Arthur Petrie, and John Skinner, on the 14th of November, 1784, he was consecrated the first bishop for the continent of America.[1]

The year 1783 had an importance for Nova Scotia even greater than that which the acces-

---

[1] Bishop Seabury preached his first sermon in America, after his consecration, in Trinity Church, St. John, New Brunswick. Dr. Chandler wrote from London to his friend Isaac Wilkins in Nova Scotia, by Dr. Seabury himself: "He goes by the way of Nova Scotia for several reasons, of which the principal is, that he may see the situation of that part of his family which is in that quarter, and be able to form a judgment of the prospects before them. He will try hard to see you, but as he will not have much time to spare, he fears that he will not be able to go to Shelburne in quest of you." Boulton's "History of Westchester," p. 103.

sion of thousands of people to the population of the province gave it. On the 21st of March of that year, just four days before the meeting of the Connecticut clergymen at Woodbury, eighteen clergymen met in New York, as so many groups of men in various parts of the country had met before, to discuss their plan for securing for America the historic episcopate. This time the scheme had not direct relation to either New England, the Middle States, or the South, but rather to the remote province of Nova Scotia, where already many of the Church's warmest supporters in the now independent colonies had taken refuge, and whither some of themselves contemplated soon removing. These clergymen were: the Reverend Charles Inglis, D.D., Rector of Trinity Church, New York, Reverend H. Addison, of St. John's, Maryland, Reverend Jonathan Odell, Missionary at Burlington and Mt. Holly, New Jersey, Reverend Benjamin Moore, D.D., Assistant Minister of Trinity Church, New York, Reverend Charles Mongan, Reverend Samuel Seabury, D.D., Missionary at Staten Island, New York, Reverend Jeremiah Leaming, Missionary, late at Norwalk, Connecticut, Reverend I. Waller, Reverend Moses Badger, S. P. G. Itinerant Missionary in New Hampshire, Reverend George Panton, Missionary at Trenton, New Jersey, Reverend John Beardsley, Missionary at Poughkeepsie, New York, Reverend Isaac Browne, Missionary at Newark, New Jersey, Reverend John Sayre, Missionary, late at Fairfield, Connecticut, Reverend John Hamilton Rowland, Missionary in Pennsylvania, Reverend Thomas Moore, of New York, Reverend George Bissett, Rector of Newport, Rhode Island, Reverend Joshua Bloomer, Missionary at Jamaica, Flushing, and Newtown, Long Island, and Reverend John Bowden, of Newburgh, New York. Of these eighteen clergymen, nine, as we shall see further on, went soon after to the province where they were now proposing to erect a diocese. Of the number, three, Drs. Seabury, Inglis, and Moore, became in 1784, 1787, and 1801, respectively, bishops of the newly-organizing Church in the western world. The outcome of this New York convention was a letter to Sir Guy Carleton signed by seventeen of the clergymen who composed it, dated New York, March 26, 1783, recommending for consecration to the

Nova Scotia see, Dr. Thomas Bradbury Chandler, then in England, a New Jersey clergyman, nearly fifty-seven years old, a native of Connecticut, a strong churchman and foremost among those who desired to see Episcopacy fully established in America. Dr. Chandler was in ill health, suffering from some disease of which he died in 1790, and so felt obliged to refuse the proffered bishopric, but being requested by the Archbishop of Canterbury, with whom he was on terms of friendship, to propose some other clergyman, he at once named his old friend, Dr. Charles Inglis.

THE RIGHT REVEREND CHARLES INGLIS, D.D., the first bishop of Nova Scotia, was born in or about the year 1733. His father was the Rev. Archibald Inglis, of Glen and Kilcarr, in Ireland, a clergyman of the English Church, as were also his grandfather and great grandfather. Like many other British youths, in early life he emigrated to the New World to seek a livelihood, and for several years before 1757, was in charge, or else assistant master, of the Free School, Lancaster, Pennsylvania, established by a society in England, with the Archbishop of Canterbury at its head, for the purpose of educating the children of German settlers in Pennsylvania. At last, in 1758, having been ordained to the diaconate and priesthood by the Bishop of London, and licensed to minister in Pennsylvania, he was appointed to the mission at Dover, Delaware, and in the summer of 1759, after a long and stormy passage across the Atlantic, entered upon his cure. In Bishop Perry's sermon on the centenary of the consecration of Bishop Inglis, preached in Westminster Abbey on Friday, August 12, 1887, his work in Delaware is thus described:

"In that noble collection of letters from laborers in mission fields, bound up in huge volumes on the shelves of the library of the venerable society—letters which, so far as they relate to the Church in the United States, have been carefully transcribed at the cost of that Church, and published in sumptuous volumes—and in the MS. collections at Fulham and Lambeth, there still remain the letters of this tireless missionary, this faithful parish priest. Vivid, indeed, are the pictures of clerical life and experience in America a century and more ago given in these carefully-written folios. The mission of Dover, assigned to Mr. Inglis, comprised the whole county of Kent, in Delaware, and was thirty-three miles in length, and from ten to thirteen miles in breadth. The cure included a population of seven thousand souls. The climate was unhealthy. The labor was unceasing. Three churches needing repair, lacking proper furnishings, and wanting all the accessories for reverent and fitting worship, awaited the missionary's arrival. To make these untidy structures meet for the worship of God, was the first care of the young 'missioner.' Their enlargement followed. The substitution of a more substantial edifice for one of perishable material was the next step in the advance. Still another, a fourth, church was soon required. Nor was the spiritual prosperity of the people overlooked. Soon the mission was reported to be 'in a flourishing state, if building and repairing churches, if crowds attending the public worship of God, and other religious ordinances, if some of the other denominations joining us, and the renewal of a spirit of piety can denominate it such.'[1] The zeal and faithful ministrations of

---

[1] See Perry's "Historical Collections of the American Colonial Church," v., 112.

Mr. Inglis obtained the public commendation of the great evangelist Whitefield, then making his progresses through the colonies, and at this period of his career free from many of the extravagances of his earlier years. The friendship of the leading clergy of the neighboring colonies, and the confidence and favor of the laity as well, were also secured; and on the death of his wife, and on the loss of his own health, which had been impaired from the first by the unhealthiness of the climate, Mr. Inglis reluctantly accepted an invitation to New York, where he was appointed an assistant minister of Trinity Church, and a catechist to the negroes of the city. So pleasant had been his relations with the Venerable Society, that he accepted his new appointment on condition of his continuance on the list of the Society's missionaries."

Of Bishop Inglis' early labors in New York, we learn much from Berrian's History of Trinity Parish, and from the bishop's own letters, many of which Bishop Perry has carefully transcribed and published. As missionary in Delaware he had been earnest and faithful. Now in a subordinate position, in a far different field, he soon gained an equal reputation for diligence, faithfulness, devotion to the Church's work, ability, and eloquence. Dr. Berrian in his annals of this period of the history of Trinity parish makes marked mention of "the growing estimate of the value and importance of his services."[1] He undertook a "mission of inquiry" to the Indians and made a very valuable report concerning them; he became a skilful controversialist, defending the views of his Church against the various forms of dissent; he corresponded regularly and faithfully with the S. P. G., who came to regard him as one of their most reliable missionaries, and who frequently guided their movements by his judgment, and he preached sermons so earnest and evangelical that Whitefield spoke in their praise.

In 1777, Dr. Auchmuty, Rector of Trinity Church, died and Dr. Inglis succeeded to the rectorship. The church had been burned the year before in the terrible fire in which nearly one thousand buildings in the western part of

---

[1] Berrian's "History of Trinity Parish," New York, p. 127. Also Bishop Perry's Centennial Sermon in Westminster Abbey.

New York City were destroyed,[1] and Dr. Inglis was inducted into office by placing his hands on a portion of the ruined wall,[2] in presence of the wardens, and taking the usual obligations. From letters of various missionaries to the S. P. G., we learn that when General Washington assumed command in New York, designing to attend Trinity Church, he sent word by one of his generals that he would be glad to have the rector omit the customary prayers for the king and the royal family. To this request Dr. Inglis paid no attention at the time, but when later he saw Washington, he remonstrated with him on its unreasonableness. Soon after, he was insulted and threatened with violence in the streets by Whig sympathizers, who called him a traitor to his country, his great offence being his persisting to pray for the king. At last, one Sunday morning, during service, about one-hundred and fifty men entered the church with bayonets fixed, drums beating, and fifes

---

[1] St. Paul's Chapel and King's College would have been burned at this time, save for Dr. Inglis, who, happening to be near, sent men to the roofs of both with buckets of water. This he himself tells in a valuable letter written in 1776.

[2] "By placing his hand on the wall of the said church, the same being a ruin;" is Rev. William Berrian's way of putting it.

playing, and after standing for a few minutes in the aisle were given seats in the pews. The congregation were terrified, but Dr. Inglis went quietly on with the service and as usual offered the offensive prayers, the soldiers listening, however, without remonstrance. In August, 1776, like most Episcopal clergymen throughout the disaffected colonies, having closed his church, he took refuge in Flushing, Long Island, sending his family, for safety, seventy miles up the North River. In Flushing the Whig committee discussed the question of seizing him, but for some reason he was allowed to go free, and for a time kept himself as much as possible concealed. When the royal army gained possession of New York he returned to the city, where he drew up a petition which was signed by about a thousand persons; praying His Majesty to pardon their temporary submission to the rebel forces and to receive the city again under his gracious protection. This petition was presented to Lord Howe on the 16th of October, and by him forwarded to the king. During his stay in Long Island, his house was stripped of everything of value it contained. His letters during the progress of the Revolution, show him to have been very pronounced in his sympathy with the Crown, and correspondingly bitter against the Whigs. "The present rebellion," he writes to the Society in the autumn of 1776, "is certainly one of the most causeless, unprovoked, and unnatural that ever disgraced any country." Not one of the clergy in these provinces, he says, "and very few of the laity who were respectable or men of property, have joined in the rebellion." "I have no doubt but with the blessing of Providence, His Majesty's arms will be successful, and finally crush this unnatural rebellion."

Both Dr. Inglis and his wife were included in the confiscation act of New York, and in 1783, the year of the evacuation of New York by the British troops, he went to Nova Scotia. As early as May, 1785, he was in England, where he probably remained until 1787, when, on the 12th of August, he was consecrated at Lambeth the first bishop of Nova Scotia, with jurisdiction over the provinces of Upper and Lower Canada, New Brunswick, Prince Edward Island, Bermuda, and Newfoundland. Sailing from England, he reached Halifax on Tuesday, October 16, 1787, and was received with many expressions of good will and of hopefulness for the success of the work he had undertaken.[1] In May, 1809, he was made a member of His Majesty's Council, his place to be next after the chief justice. It was declared, however, that he was not to administer the government in the absence or on the death of the lieutenant-governor. He died, February 24, 1816, in the eighty-second year of his age, the fifty-eighth of his ministry, and the twenty-ninth of his episcopate, and was buried on Thursday, February 29th, in St. Paul's Church, the Reverend William Twining, Rector of Rawdon, reading the burial service; the Governor, Sir John Coape Sherbrook, the ex-Governor, Sir John Wentworth, the members of council and of the assembly, the officers of the army and navy, the clergy and the principal inhabitants attending the funeral.

After the Bishop was made a member of the council his winter residence was in Halifax, but early in his episcopate, through the influence of Mr. James Morden, a retired officer of the

---

[1] Bishop Inglis writes in 1787 that he had received two patents, one to himself for life, making his see a bishop's see, the other during the king's pleasure.

Ordnance in Halifax, who owned a large property in Aylesford, now part of Kings County, he bought land there and built a country house, calling his place "Clermont," the name it always since has borne. In time, Bishop Inglis gave part of his Aylesford land to his daughter, Margaret, wife of Sir Brenton Halliburton, and for many years both the Bishop and Sir Brenton moved regularly from Halifax every spring, with their horses and servants, to their Aylesford homes, a distance of about ninety miles. When the bishop died he willed Clermont to his son John, fixing the entail in the next generation, on his grandson, Charles. Later, this property came into possession of King's College. Sir Brenton Halliburton willed his part of the Aylesford property to his son John, who sold it.[1]

---

[1] When the Duke of Kent arrived in Halifax in 1794 the Bishop, on behalf of himself and his clergy, presented him with an address which, it must be confessed, is rather bombastic. At some time during the Duke's stay in Halifax the Bishop fell from his horse and broke his leg. The Duke hearing of it, sent a deputation of soldiers all the way to Aylesford, bearing a large comfortable English arm-chair for his use. This chair is still in Aylesford in the possession of a Mrs. Rutherford. The Reverend Richard Avery, long Rector of Aylesford, now of Kentville, has a table, flute, microscope, and paper-knife of the first Bishop Inglis, as well as steel engravings of

In 1767 Bishop Inglis received from King's College, New York, the honorary degree of M.A., and three years later became a governor of the college. A few years after, he received the same degree from Oxford, which university, in 1778, also conferred on him the degree of D.D. His published writings were very few. In 1776, he published an answer to Paine's "Common Sense," which Sabine says the Whigs seized and burned, two editions of it, however, being printed afterward in Philadelphia. He published also an essay on Infant Baptism, a "Vindication of the Bishop of Llandaff's Sermon," and two or three letters and sermons. During his seventeen years' ministry in Trinity Church, New York, he married nine hundred and twenty-five couples. On the death, in 1774, of Dr. John Ogilvie, for nine years his colleague, he preached an eloquent and feeling funeral sermon, performing the same office in 1777 for his rector, Dr. Auchmuty, with whom

---

both father and son. Bishop Charles Inglis had a fine library which after his son John's death was sent to England and sold. This library contained among other things a full set of the early reports of the S.P.G., which so far as is known, no library in this country now contains. It is most unfortunate that they were lost to the Province.

he had been associated for twelve years. His first wife, whom he married soon after he went to Delaware, was a Miss Vining, who died without children in 1764. It was her ill health, he writes, that decided him to leave his Delaware mission. His second wife was Margaret, daughter of John Crooke, Esquire, of Ulster County, New York, who died in 1783, the year of his going to Nova Scotia, aged thirty-five, leaving four young children, a son who died at nine years of age, John, Margaret, and Anne. In November, 1776, during the Revolutionary troubles, Mrs. Inglis was at New Windsor, whence she wrote asking Mr. Duane to procure leave for her to join her husband in New York "with her family and effects." She had been absent from him, she said, nearly fourteen months, had three helpless babes, and was greatly distressed. The Bishop's family at this time, besides his wife and children, is said to have consisted of his mother-in-law, Mrs. Crooke, two white servant women, a nurse, and a white servant boy, all of whom at length joined him, under a flag of truce. Of his chilren, John became the third bishop of Nova Scotia, Margaret was married, September 19,

1799, to Sir Brenton Halliburton, Chief Justice of Nova Scotia, and Anne was married to the Reverend George Pidgeon, for many years rector of Fredericton, New Brunswick, and afterwards of St. John. Mrs. Pidgeon died at Halifax in 1827, aged fifty-one. Sir Brenton Halliburton describes his father-in-law as a gentleman of the old school, dignified but not formal, with a slight figure and an open, intelligent countenance. In preaching he had great energy and earnestness, he says, and in conversation was cheerful and communicative. He was of studious habits and was well read, but was free from pedantry.

Not the least interesting part of Bishop Inglis' correspondence, are his letters to Bishop White, of Pennsylvania, both before and after the latter's consecration. He had long been one of the foremost advocates of the establishment of the Episcopate in America, and not content with aiding by word and pen the efforts of Connecticut Churchmen to get consecration for Dr. Seabury, he gave judicious counsel and valuable help to the clergy of the Middle States in their efforts to secure bishops in the English line. It is needless to say that with the scheme of a Presbyterian Episcopal Church, for a time favored by Dr. White, he had no sympathy.

Of the Bishop's work in his own diocese, something more will appear in a later chapter. In his sermon in Westminster Abbey, Bishop Perry has thus summed it up:

"Gathering his clergy together for counsel and personal knowledge, the Bishop of Nova Scotia proved himself to be a missionary apostle by the wisdom of his charges and sermons, and the magnetism of his personal interest in each one who had been placed under him in the Lord. In long and most wearisome visitations he visited, so far as was in his power, the various portions of his almost illimitable See, and till the close of a long and honored life he maintained that character for devotion, that reputation for holiness, that fervor of ministrations, that faithfulness in every good word and work, which should characterize the 'good man,' 'full of the Holy Ghost and of faith.' Nor was this all. Through his long and earnest labors, ended only when the summons came to depart and be at rest, 'much people were added to the Lord.' A church was organized; a college was founded and built up to a measure of efficiency and success. The institutions of religion and learning were thus established and supported. The preaching of the Word and the ministration of the Sacraments were provided for the crowds of exiles who, in their devotion to Church and State, had exchanged their American homes for the bleak shores of Nova Scotia, and to the frontier settlers in the dense forests of New Brunswick and Quebec. Thus through unremitting labors, blessed by God, ere the life of the first Colonial Bishop was ended there had been set on foot measures for the development of the Church of Christ in the northern portion of the American Continent which shall act and react for good till time shall be no more."

Reverend Thomas Bradbury Chandler, D.D., the first clergyman nominated for the Nova Scotia See, was the son of William and Jemima (Bradbury) Chandler. He was born in Woodstock, Connecticut, April 26, 1726, graduated at Yale College in 1745, and received from Oxford the degrees of M.A., and D.D., the latter in 1766. Bred a Congregationalist, in 1751, he went to England for Holy Orders and was at once appointed to the mission at Elizabethtown, New Jersey, which also included Woodbridge. In 1767, he published and dedicated to the Archbishop of Canterbury an "Appeal to the public in behalf of the Church of England in America; wherein the Origin and Nature of the Episcopal Office are briefly considered, Reasons for sending Bishops to America are assigned, the Plan on which it is proposed to send them is stated, and the Objections against sending them are obviated and confuted. With an appendix wherein is given some account of an anonymous pamphlet." This pamphlet was spiritedly answered in the New York *Gazette*, and the Pennsylvania *Journal*, and by Rev. Dr. Chauncey, in a pamphlet with a title nearly as long-winded as that of Dr. Chandler's. Before the Revolution Dr. Chandler, who was an uncompromising Loyalist, tried by voice and pen to avert the coming conflict. Then he went to England where he remained from 1775 to 1785. In England he lived in intercourse with the Archbishop of Canterbury, and other dignitaries of the Church, and noblemen, and while there was elected bishop of Nova Scotia. His letter to the Archbishop of Canterbury declining the honor was answered by his Lordship in a most friendly way. In a short time, by request of his parishioners in New Jersey, who seem still to have regarded him as their rector, Dr. Chandler returned to Elizabethtown, and resumed the rectorship of St. John's Church, although, owing to a cancer on the nose, he never officiated except at one or two funerals. He died in 1790. His wife was Jane, daughter of Captain John Emmott, of Elizabethtown, who died September 20, 1801, aged sixty-eight. General Maxwell, in a communication to the legislature in 1779, said of her: "There is not a Tory that passes in or out of New Jersey . . . but waits on Mrs. Chandler, and most of all the British officers going in or out on parole or exchange, wait on her; in short, the governor, the whole of the Tories, and many of the Whigs." Dr. Chandler "was large and portly, of fine personal appearance, of a countenance expressive of high intelligence though considerably marred by the small-pox, with an uncommonly fine blue eye, a strong, commanding voice, and a great love of music." He and Mrs. Chandler had a family of six children. One of their daughters was the wife of General E. B. Dayton, and another of Bishop Hobart, the third bishop of New York.

CHAPTER VIII.

THE CHURCH AT SHELBURNE.

IN any review of Loyalist times in Nova Scotia, the history of the town and church of Shelburne demands more than a passing notice. Early in the Revolution, Captain Gideon White of Plymouth, visited Shelburne, then called Port Roseway, and advised his fellow Loyalists to settle there. So favorably was his advice looked upon, that before long a considerable number of New York men got together and formed a plan for a new city at Port Roseway, which should be a Loyalist stronghold, and should quickly rival Halifax, the Nova Scotia capital. April 27, 1783, there set sail from New York a fleet of sixteen square-rigged ships and several sloops and schooners, protected by two ships of war, containing four hundred and seventy-one families, with Beverly Robinson at their head. On the 4th of May these people reached Port Roseway, where they were met by three surveyors from

Halifax, with whose aid they at once began to plan their town. The plan made provision for five parallel streets, sixty feet wide, to be intersected by others at right angles, each square to contain sixteen lots, sixty feet in width, and one hundred and twenty feet in depth. At each end of the town a large space was left for a common, and these reservations the engineers, with the assistance of fatigue parties, rapidly cleared so that tents could be erected for the temporary shelter of the people. July 11th, the town was divided into north and south, the streets were named and the lots numbered, every settler being given fifty acres on each side the harbor, and a town and water lot. From 1784, Shelburne occupied a position as a naval and military station, next to Halifax; ships of war were always anchored in its harbor, and a regiment was quartered in the town. In 1786, says Murdoch, the new city "was a gay and lively place. Every holiday or anniversary of any description was loyally kept and mirthfully enjoyed. On St. Andrews Day, December 11, 1786, the St. Andrews Society gave an elegant ball, at the merchants' coffee house.

The ball-room was crowded on the occasion and the hours of the night passed away in the most pleasing manner." As soon as the people were well established, Governor Parr paid them a visit, arriving off Point Carleton, on Sunday, the 20th of July, in His Majesty's sloop, "La Sophie." The 14th of May, 1784, Sir Charles Douglas, Bart., Commander-in-Chief of the Navy on the North American station, also came, and the 25th of May, Sir John Wentworth, Governor Parr repeating his visit the same summer.[1] Four years later, Shelburne was visited by no less illustrious a person than Prince William Henry, afterwards King William IV., who arrived in the war ship "Andromeda," and stayed four days. During his short visit a ball was given in his honor, which the Prince opened with Mrs. Bruce, wife of the collector of the port. In July, 1790, Bishop Inglis visited the town, consecrated Christ Church, and confirmed two hundred and seventy-six persons, "besides eight negroes." This first visit of Bishop Inglis to Shelburne must have had more than common interest, for the newly consecrated prelate, of

[1] Murdoch, vol. 3, chapter III.

course, found there not a few of his old New York parishioners, from whom he had been separated for fourteen eventful years.

The ultimate fate of the Shelburne settlement is told by Bishop John Inglis, in a letter written by him in 1844. "I have lately been at Shelburne," he writes, "where nearly ten thousand loyalists, chiefly from New York, and comprising many of my father's parishioners, attracted by the beauty and security of a most noble harbor, were tempted to plant themselves, regardless of the important want of any country in the neighborhood fit for cultivation. Their means were soon exhausted in building a spacious town, at great expense, and vainly contending against indomitable rocks; and in a few years the place was reduced to a few hundred families. Many of these returned to their native country, and a large portion of them were reduced to poverty. . . . Some few of the first emigrants are still living. I visited these aged members of the Church. They told me that on their first arrival, lines of women could be seen sitting on the rocks of the shore, and weeping at their altered condition."

The Church at Shelburne. 139

Soon after the arrival of the Loyalists at Shelburne, a temporary building was put up for worship, and subscriptions were begun towards the erection of a permanent church. The first clergyman known to have officiated in the new town was Dr. William Walter, formerly rector of Trinity Church, Boston, who in 1776 left that city for England, but afterwards returned to New York, and in 1783, possibly with the April fleet, with his family of six persons, accompanied by three servants, went to Shelburne. The preserved record of his ministry in the Loyalist town begins in August, 1783. In July of that year, the Reverend George Panton, a New Jersey clergyman, and the Reverend John Sayre, formerly of Fairfield, Connecticut, were among the fifty-nine petitioners for lands in Nova Scotia, and soon after, Mr. Panton also went to Shelburne. Dr. Walter was in Boston, it is said, from December, 1783, to November, 1784, and it is possible that this clergyman may have officiated in his absence. Before August, 1786, the Reverend John Hamilton Rowland, of Pennsylvania, arrived in Shelburne, and soon two parishes were made, Dr. Walter being appointed rector of St. George's, and Mr. Rowland of St. Patrick's. Unhappily, at first, there was not perfect good feeling between these two parishes, but in May, 1788, at the first parish meeting in Shelburne of which we have any record, the rectors and vestries of both parishes being present, a vote of thanks to the Venerable Society was passed, for its "munificence and condescension in granting to the town a mission for each of the gentlemen settled there as rectors of the two parishes, by means of which those differences which formerly did exist among the members of the Church are happily done away, and union and harmony restored." The next Sunday, Mr. Rowland preached "an admirable sermon" from the text: "We took sweet counsel together, and walked in the house of God as friends."

At the meeting referred to, steps were also taken for a more permanent and church-like building for worship, the British Government having offered a generous sum for that purpose. Tenders being soon called for, at an adjourned meeting, June 6, 1788, the tender of Messrs. Hildreth and White for the sum of six hundred and twenty pounds was accepted, four hundred pounds of this sum to be given by the Home Government. The contract was executed in June, 1788, and the building was handed over to the wardens, completed "in a handsome and workman-like manner, and of excellent materials," in December, 1789. In the mean time, however, the Marquis of Lansdowne and Earl of Shelburne, from whom the place received its name, had been appealed to for aid in completing the building, and Sir Charles Douglas had been asked for the bell of the "Ville de Paris," the French admiral, Count de Grasse's flag ship, captured April 12, 1782, when the great victory over the French, under Lord Rodney, was won. The bell had been otherwise disposed of, but the Marquis of Lansdowne gave the church twenty guineas, and Sir William Pepperell ten, the people themselves contributing at least two hundred pounds. At the completion of the church, the church-wardens report, that "agreeable to the order of the committee, at last meeting, they had taken seizure and possession of the said church, from the said contract builders in the name and behalf, and to the use of the two parishes, in due form of law, by receiving at the hands of the said Hildreth and White, the key of the great west door of the church, turning out the said builders, and locking the door upon them, and then immediately opening the door again." This was on the 22d of December, 1789, and the first service was held the following Christmas day. The church under the name of Christ Church, and the churchyard, were consecrated by Bishop Inglis, as we have seen, on Friday, July 30, 1790, the sermon, by direction of the bishop, since Dr. Walter was in Boston, being preached by Mr. Rowland. Dr. Walter finally left the parish at Easter, 1791, and Mr. Rowland became sole rector of the two parishes, which on the 10th of May, 1793, were joined under the name of "The United Parishes of St. George and St. Patrick." Early in 1795, Mr. Rowland becoming very ill, he earnestly asked Bishop Inglis to ordain his son, Thomas Bolby Rowland, then a student at King's College. The bishop at once complied, and February 11, 1795, Mr. Rowland, Junior, was introduced to the wardens and vestry by his father, then on his death bed. The father died shortly after, in his forty-fourth year, and on the 26th of February the son officiated at his funeral. In due time Thomas Rowland was admitted to the priesthood, and October 9, 1795, was appointed rector of the united parishes. He married (the Reverend Benjamin Gerrish Gray of Preston, Halifax County, officiating) Miss Braine, eldest daughter of Mr. Thomas Braine. Like his father, he was a good, intelligent, faithful pastor, but in 1835, feeling the infirmities of age upon him, he asked for an assistant and, January 1, 1836, the present aged rector, the Reverend Thomas Howland White, ordained in 1829, a son of Captain Gideon White, was appointed missionary in charge. Dr. Rowland left for the United States in 1846, and died a few years afterward in Pittsburg, Pennsylvania, having been for fifty-one years rector of the parish.

July 30, 1890, the centennial of the consecration of Christ Church, Shelburne, was observed, the venerable Dr. White, in the eighty-fifth year, of his age, the sixty-second of his ministry, and the fifty-fifth of his incumbency at Shelburne, preaching an able historical memorial sermon. In this sermon, Dr. White says of the first Shelburne clergyman: "Dr. William Walter has been described to me by those who knew him as a 'good preacher, a diligent pastor, and a pious man, much beloved by his people.' In his farewell address he speaks of the 'painfulness of leaving a people among whom he had long (nine years) and happily labored. He alludes also to the handsome set of books, and valuable silver communion plate, obtained from a gentleman in London.'" Of Reverend John Hamilton Rowland, Dr. White says: He was "a learned man and a good preacher. In writing to the bishop recommending the Reverend Thomas Bolby Rowland as his father's successor, the wardens and vestry speak of their mournful loss in the death of their much-regretted, benevolent, and truly pious rector. It is but justice to say that he performed every duty with the truest sincerity and zeal, at once being an ornament and example of the Christian character."

At the close of the eighteenth century, the population of Shelburne was only about seven hundred, but later, it became a town of rather more importance. It has always been known as a place of intelligence and refinement, many of the best of its people, like their Tory ancestors, being devout members of the Church.

CHAPTER IX.

THE NEW TORY PROVINCE.

THE settlement of the province of New Brunswick, like the settlement of Upper Canada, is conspicuously a result of the American Revolution. Before that event both provinces were almost uninhabited, except for the wandering tribes of Indians, the smoke from whose scattered wigwams rose heavenward from the shore of many a lake and stream in the dense virgin forest. The Loyalist emigration to the Nova Scotia woods, both in its causes and in the character of the people who composed it, is certainly unique in history. The emigration is sometimes spoken of as if it had been impelled merely by excess of sentiment, and was in the main a voluntary movement. But this is not true. If it had not been for the fierce legislation of the Whigs in the various colonies against the adherents of the crown, the history of this part of the country, both secular and religious, would be vastly different from what it is. In New York, New Hampshire, Massachusetts, Rhode Island, Connecticut, Pennsylvania, Virginia, Maryland, and the Carolinas, acts of such severity were passed against the sympathizers with Britain, that when the issue of the conflict was decided, longer residence for them in the revolting colonies was practically impossible. So, stripped of their estates, proscribed by the new laws, and in some cases fresh from prison, with the aid of the British commander, Sir Guy Carleton, they sadly sought new British soil on which to plant themselves.

The attention of the New York Loyalists seems to have been early directed towards the almost uninhabited province of New Brunswick, then known as the County of Sunbury, a part of His Majesty's loyal province of Nova Scotia. In the beginning of 1783, says Murdoch, Amos Botsford and some others, whom the Loyalists had sent from New York to explore the country, wrote from Annapolis Royal to their friends, of the beauty of Annapolis Basin, St. Mary's Bay, and the river St. John, which they represent as equal in size to the Connecticut or the Hudson.

They also describe minutely the harbor, the port, the intervale land along the Kennebecasis, and the few inhabitants already in the country, and give much encouragement to their fellow Loyalists to settle there. Accordingly, in April, a fleet of twenty vessels left New York for the River St. John, having on board three thousand Loyalists, men, women, and children, who, in October, were joined at St. John by twelve hundred persons, who came in the fall fleet, and others who came in single vessels. In all, it is estimated, at least five thousand persons passed the winter of 1783-84 on the site of the new city, many of whom in the spring received land in other parts of the province, and moved to their new homes. New Brunswick was created a separate province in 1784, and the city of St. John was chartered in 1785.[1]

---

[1] The chief Acadian fort next to Port Royal was Fort la Tour, on the River St. John. It was there that Charles la Tour, when the whole of Acadia was divided between him and his rival, d'Aulnay Charnisé, had his headquarters; there that that heroic woman, "Constance of Acadia," Madame la Tour, in the absence of her lord, with a handful of soldiers bravely defending her husband's rights, earned for herself a lasting fame. When Acadia came finally under British rule, another fort, called Fort Howe, was built on the opposite side of the river, not far away from which grew up the city of St. John.

The English settlers in New Brunswick in 1782 did not number over a thousand, five hundred of whom lived in the settlements of Maugerville, Burton, and Gagetown, along the River St. John. Like so many of the old inhabitants of Nova Scotia, these people had come from New England long before Revolutionary troubles began; but, as we learn from old documents, they were not New England farmers, but rather, chiefly, disbanded provincial officers and soldiers, who had served in various campaigns, and now desired a settled agricultural life.[1] To these people, as to the

---

[1] An interesting old manuscript, formerly in the possession of the Perleys of Fredericton, describes the first English settlement of New Brunswick as follows:

"In the year 1761 a number of DISBANDED Provincial officers and soldiers in New England who had servd. in several Campains During the then french war agreed to form a settlement on St. John River in Nova Scotia, for which Purpose they sent one of their number to Halifax who obtained an order of Survey for Laying out a Township in miles squares in any part of St. John's River (the whole being then a Desolate wilderness). This Township called magerville was laid out in the year 1761 [or 1762?] and a number of settlers entered into it; Encouraged by the King's Proclamation for settling the land in Nova Scotia in which among other things was this clause that People emigrating from the New England Provinces to Nova Scotia should enjoy the same Religious Priviledges as in New England—and in the above-mentioned order of Survey was the following words—viz., 'you shall Reserve four Lots

Indians in New Brunswick, that indefatigable missionary, the Reverend Thomas Wood, had made a visit from Annapolis in 1769, but with the exception of occasional services held by Mr. Eagleson, in Westmoreland County, near his Cumberland mission, there is no record of any other Church clergyman's visiting the province, until the arrival at St. John with their fellow Loyalists, in 1783, of the Reverend John Sayre, and the Reverend John Beardsley, well-known clergymen of the Church in the older colonies. Mr. Sayre did not stay long at

---

in the Township for Publick use, one as a Glebe for the Church of England, one for the Dissenting Protestant; one for the maintenance of a School, and for the first settled minister in Place.' These orders were strictly complyd with IN THE YEAR 1763, but finding Difficulty in obtaining a Grant of this Township from the government of Nova Scotia on account of an order from home that those Lands should be Reservd. for Disbanded forces, the settlers Did in the year 1763 Draw up and forwarded a Petition to the Lords of Trade and Plantations setting forth the *services they had Done* for government in *the last war*. The encourage*ment they received* for Removing to *Nova Scotia at a* great expense, the*ir efforts for* bringing forwd. a *survey of the land* and Praying for a *grant of land* which they had settled."

The fact of these colonists being disbanded soldiers is important, and serves to differentiate this colony from others founded in Nova Scotia about the same time. A writer in the *Magazine of American History* for February, 1891, says they came from Byfield, Ipswich, Rowley, Boxford, and Marblehead.

St. John, but before winter set in, moved sixty miles up the river, to the settlement of Maugerville, where he preached in the Congregational meeting house to a company of old settlers and refugees. Mr. Beardsley, however, stayed at St. John, but at Mr. Sayre's death, the next year, he also went to Maugerville, where, and at Burton and other out-lying stations, he labored faithfully until 1802, St. John remaining without a missionary until the arrival of Dr. Samuel Cooke in September, 1785.

This was the beginning of the Church in New Brunswick, and these Loyalist clergymen were its pioneer missionaries. To their number must be added, also, the name of "the Honorable and Reverend" Jonathan Odell, who, although on the formation of the new province in 1784 he assumed the post of provincial secretary, and became active in the government,[1] in the absence of a missionary at

---

[1] The first officers of the new province were: Governor, Colonel Thomas Carleton, a brother of Sir Guy; Provincial Secretary, Rev. Jonathan Odell; Chief Justice, Judge George Duncan Ludlow, of New York; Judges, James Putnam, of Massachusetts, Isaac Allen, of New Jersey, and Joshua Upham of Massachusetts; Attorney-General, Daniel Bliss, of Massachusetts.

St. John, often performed the service for his fellow Churchmen.

The third Loyalist missionary to New Brunswick was the Reverend Dr. Samuel Cooke, of New Jersey, whose long, arduous labor in the province earned for him the title of "the father of the Church of England in New Brunswick." In 1774 he went to England, where he remained until August, 1785, when he sailed for Halifax on his way to his new field. September 2d, he reached St. John, where he found awaiting him, not only an expectant and kindly congregation, but a temporary house of worship, which he at once set to work to make more comfortable, until a new church could be built. From St. John he soon made a missionary tour to Campobello Island, St. Andrews, and Digdeguash, where he found Church people longing for services, and where he baptized many children and adults. At St. John, Dr. Cooke remained until August, 1786, when, the seat of government being removed to Fredericton, he was transferred to that place, where he labored until his sudden death in 1795. He was followed at St. John by the Reverend George Bissett, formerly of Trinity Church,

Newport, and at Fredericton by the Reverend George Pidgeon, a son-in-law of Bishop Inglis. In May, 1786, three more clergymen came to New Brunswick from Connecticut; the Reverend Richard Clarke, who went to Gagetown, the Reverend Samuel Andrews, who went to St. Andrews, and the Reverend James Scovil, who went to Kingston. A little later was founded the mission of Woodstock, whose first minister was the Reverend Frederick Dibblee, ordained deacon by Bishop Inglis in 1791; the mission of Westfield, whose first minister was the Reverend Robert Norris, an Englishman, formerly a priest of the Roman Catholic Church, who came to New Brunswick in 1801; and the mission of St. Stephen, under the jurisdiction of the minister of Gagetown. In 1789, Dr. Mather Byles came to St. John, assuming the rectorship of Trinity Church and the chaplaincy of the garrison, which double post he held until his death, in March, 1814. For twelve years, already, he had been garrison chaplain and assistant to Dr. Breynton at Halifax, and the advent of so distinguished a clergyman was of no small importance to the rising New Brunswick Church. Under his ministry the parish of Trinity Church, St. John, rose to a position of much dignity and influence in the new Loyalist colony. At the close of the century Dr. Byles reports that his church is crowded with earnest people, and that he has built a decent parsonage; Dr. Cooke reports at Fredericton a large congregation; while from Mr. Beardsley at Maugerville, Mr. Scovil at Kingston, Mr. Andrews at St. Andrews, and Mr. Clarke at Gagetown, come similar reports of good work done, and of growing interest in religion and the Church.

From the beginning of the century until 1845, the work of the Church in the new province went steadily on, the bishops of Nova Scotia keeping the oversight of it, and making annual tours throughout this part of their vast spiritual domain. At last it was felt that the diocese must be divided, and in 1845, the present Metropolitan of Canada, the venerable Bishop John Medley, was consecrated bishop of Fredericton, his see including the whole Tory province. This bishop was born in London, December 19, 1804, graduated at Oxford in 1826, and ordained priest in 1829. In 1838, he became vicar of St. Thomas', Exeter, and prebendary of the cathedral there, from which preferment he was called to the diocese of Fredericton. In 1864 he received the degree of Doctor of Divinity, and in 1879, became Metropolitan of Canada.

CHAPTER X.

EXILED CLERGY OF THE REVOLUTION.

THE brief biographies in this chapter contain the leading facts in the lives of that interesting group of men, the Loyalist clergymen who went to Nova Scotia and New Brunswick between 1776 and 1786. Some of them, as will be seen, soon returned to the United States, or else took passage for England, but not a few remained for the rest of their lives in the old Acadian province by the sea. The names of these clergymen have never been gathered together before, and it is possible that after the evacuation of Boston, still others may have gone with the fleet to Halifax, whose names are not recorded here. The list as compiled is as follows:

Rev. John Agnew.
Rev. Samuel Andrews.
Rev. Oliver Arnold.
Rev. Moses Badger.
Rev. Jacob Bailey.

Rev. John Beardsley.
Rev. George Bissett.
Rev. Isaac Browne.
Rev. Edward Brudenell.
Rev. Mather Byles.
Rev. Henry Caner.
Rev. Richard Samuel Clarke.
Rev. William Clarke.
Rev. Samuel Cooke.
Rev. Nathaniel Fisher.
Rev. Bernard Michael Houseal.
Rev. Charles Inglis.
Rev. John Rutgers Marshall.
Rev. —— Meff.
Rev. Jonathan Odell.
Rev. George Panton.
Rev. John Hamilton Rowland.
Rev. James Sayre.
Rev. John Sayre.
Rev. James Scovil.
Rev. Epenetus Townsend.
Rev. Roger Viets.
Rev. William Walter.
Rev. Joshua Wingate Weeks.
Rev. Isaac Wilkins.
Rev. John Wiswell.

Exiled Clergy of the Revolution. 157

The following clergymen, except Mr. Pidgeon, were born in the United States before the Revolution, and later took orders and labored in the diocese of Nova Scotia. Mr. Pidgeon, who married the younger daughter of Bishop Charles Inglis, was born in Kilkenny, Ireland, and educated at Trinity College, Dublin. Entering the army he joined the Rifles as ensign, and with them went to America at the time of the war. After the Revolution he went to Nova Scotia and studied for the Church.

Rev. James Bissett.
Rev. Frederick Dibblee.
Rev. Benjamin Gerrish Gray.
Rev. Archibald Peane Inglis.
Rev. John Inglis.
Rev. John Millidge.
Rev. George Pidgeon.
Rev. Thomas Bolby Rowland.
Rev. Elias Scovil.
Rev. Charles Wingate Weeks.

REVEREND JOHN AGNEW.

Reverend John Agnew was rector of the parish of Suffolk, Virginia. On the 24th of March, 1775, the Whig Committee called him to account for his loyalty. He soon after left that part of the country and became chaplain of the Queen's Rangers. Later, he settled in New Brunswick and died near Fredericton, in 1812, aged eighty-five. He, Stair Agnew, who was probably his son, and others, during the Revolution were taken prisoners and carried to France, but were soon brought back to America.

REVEREND SAMUEL ANDREWS, M.A.

Reverend Samuel Andrews came from Wallingford, Connecticut, in 1786. He was graduated at Yale College in 1759, and ordained by the Bishop of London in 1760. After a ministry of fifty-eight years, over thirty of which were spent at St. Andrews, New Brunswick, where he was the first minister, he died at St. Andrews, September 26, 1818, aged eighty-two. His wife, Hannah, died there January 1, 1816, aged seventy-five.

REVEREND OLIVER ARNOLD, M.A.

Reverend Oliver Arnold was a native of Connecticut, and was graduated at Yale College in 1776. At the peace he became a grantee of St. John, and for some years filled secular positions. He was ordained by Bishop Inglis, August 19, 1792, and was appointed to Sussex, New Brunswick, where he died in 1834, at the age of seventy-nine. He is said to have been a man of peculiarly sweet temper.

REVEREND MOSES BADGER, M.A.

Reverend Moses Badger was a graduate of Harvard of 1761, and some years before the war was a missionary in New Hampshire. In 1776, he went to Halifax, but before long returned to New York, where he became chaplain to De Lancey's second battalion. After the Revolution he was rector of King's Chapel, Providence, dying in that city in 1792. His wife was a daughter of Judge Saltonstall of Massachusetts, and sister of the Loyalists, Colonel Richard, and Leverett Saltonstall.

REVEREND JACOB BAILEY, M.A.

Reverend Jacob Bailey, known as "the Frontier Missionary," was born in Rowley, Massachusetts, in 1731, entered Harvard College in 1751, and graduated in 1755, in the same class with President John Adams. For a time he taught school in Kingston, and Hampton, New Hampshire. Then he preached for some years as a Congregational minister, but at last, January 10, 1760, he went to England for Holy Orders. He was ordained deacon by the Bishop of Rochester, March 2d, and priest by the Bishop of Peterboro', March 16th of that year, and was at once appointed missionary to Pownalboro, Maine, where he began his work July 1st. He married, in August, 1761, Sally, daughter of Dr. John Weeks, of Hampton, New Hampshire, who had been his pupil, and was much younger than he. In 1779, he, his wife, and his three children, a young infant, and two girls of about eleven years, in a deplorable condition went to Halifax, where they were most hospitably received by the good Dr. Breynton, and Mr. Bailey was soon given an appointment to Cornwallis by the S. P. G. Later he became missionary at Annapolis, where he died in 1808. During the last twenty-six years of his life he was absent from his church but one Sunday. His wife died at Annapolis in 1818, aged seventy. His eldest son, Charles Percey, who was remarkable for personal beauty, was a captain in the British army, and was killed at the battle of Chippewa, in the war of 1812. His son, William Gilbert, was a lawyer of wide practice and died young, leaving a family. His son, Thomas Henry, was an officer in the militia and also died young, leaving a family. His daughters were Charlotte Maria, and Elizabeth Anna, who became the wife of a Mr. Whitman.

REVEREND JOHN BEARDSLEY, M.A.

Reverend John Beardsley was born at Ripton, Connecticut, in 1732. He was a student at Yale College, but did not graduate. Kings (Columbia) College, however, conferred on him the degrees of B.A. and M.A. In 1761 he went to England for orders, returned the next year, and for five years ministered at Norwich and Groton. When the war broke out he was at Poughkeepsie and Fishkill, and having declared himself on the British side, Colonel Beverley Robinson, who had been one of his chief supporters, appointed him chaplain of the Loyal American Regiment which he commanded. At the evacuation of New York, Mr. Beardsley accompanied the regiment to New Brunswick, and after "many deprivations and sufferings," was settled over the parish in Maugerville, on the St. John River, where he remained for more than seventeen years. He finally retired from the parish on account of infirmity, and went to Kingston, New Brunswick, on chaplain's half pay. There he died in 1810. He had four daughters and at least two sons. His eldest daughter was married to a German officer; his youngest son, Hon. Bartholemew Crannel Beardsley, who died in Upper Canada in 1855, was chief judge of the court of common pleas, and a member of the house of assembly of New Brunswick.

REVEREND GEORGE BISSETT.

Reverend George Bissett came from England and was employed as assistant in Trinity Church, Newport, and school-master, in 1767. October 28, 1771, he succeeded Rev. Arthur Browne as Rector of Trinity Church, continuing in office until the evacuation of Newport by the British troops, October 25, 1779. He then went with the army to New York, leaving his wife and child, it is said, very destitute. His furniture was seized, but soon restored to Mrs. Bissett, who got leave from the General

Assembly to join her husband. "Soon after his departure the church was entered and the altar-piece—ornamented with emblems of royalty—was torn down and spoiled." In 1786, he was in England. Thence he sailed for New Brunswick, and landed at St. John late in July. The *Royal Gazette* of August 1, 1786, says: "Last Sunday morning the Rev. Geo. Bissett, lately arrived from England, preached in the Church in this City, and in the evening Messrs. Moore and Gibbons, of the people called Quakers, the former from New Jersey, the latter from Pennsylvania. The whole gave great satisfaction." The Rev. Dr. Samuel Peters said of Mr. Bissett: "He is a very sensible man, a good scholar and compiler of sermons, although too bashful to appear in company, or in the pulpit." He died March 3, 1788, leaving a widow and one son. His wife was Penelope, daughter of Judge James Honyman of the Court of Vice-Admiralty, Rhode Island.

REVEREND ISAAC BROWNE, M.A.

Reverend Isaac Browne was the third son of Daniel Browne of West Haven, Conn., and brother of Reverend Daniel Browne who graduated at Yale College in 1714. Isaac Browne was born March 20, 1708-9, and graduated at Yale College in 1729. After graduation he pursued his theological studies under the direction of his brother's classmate and friend, Reverend Samuel Johnson of Stratford, who mentioned him to the secretary of the S. P. G., in June, 1731, as a "virtuous and discreet young man and of good abilities." He began as school-master and reader in the village of Setauket, in Brooklyn, Long Island, to a small Episcopal congregation. In 1733, he went to England, and was ordained deacon and priest, returning again to his Brooklyn congregation. In 1744, he was transferred to Newark, N. J., where he continued till the Revolution. He also practised as a physician, and was elected to the New Jersey Medical Society, November, 1766. At the close of 1776, he took refuge within the British lines, and in 1783, went to Annapolis, Nova Scotia, having a tempestuous voyage and losing most of his goods. He was too old and feeble for work, and the S. P. G. allowed him a pension of £50 a year. He died in Nova Scotia in 1787. His wife had been made delirious by the voyage and she too soon died. One of their sons was a surgeon in the British army. One daughter married a son of David Ogden.

REVEREND MR. BRUDENELL.

The Reverend Mr. Brudenell was a chaplain of the Artillery under General Burgoyne, and is described in Jones' "History of New York during the Revolution," as having, amidst great danger, performed the burial service over the body of General Frazer, who died October 9, 1777, as a result of the engagement of October 7th. In November, 1784, he was one of the four persons authorized by the governor to lay out and assign unlocated lands in Digby.

REVEREND MATHER BYLES, D.D.

Mather Byles, Junior, D.D., was a son of the Reverend Mather Byles, D.D., first pastor of the Hollis Street Church, Boston, on his mother's side descended from Richard Mather and John Cotton. Mather Byles, Junior, was born in Boston in 1734, and graduated at Harvard College in 1751. In 1757, he was ordained at New London to the ministry of the Congregaional Church, his father preaching the sermon. "Eleven years after, his ministry came to an abrupt termination. Without previous intimation, he called a meeting of his church, and requested dismission, that he might accept an invitation to become rector of the North, or Christ Church, Salem Street, Boston. His congregation was much displeased and the record on the church books, April 12, 1768, is: "The Rev. Mr. Byles dismissed himself from the church and congregation." Before the close of 1768, he was inducted into the rectorship of Christ Church, of which he was the third rector. In 1776, with his family of four persons, he went to Halifax, and in 1778 was proscribed and banished. Soon after his arrival in Halifax, he was appointed garrison chaplain. He also assisted Dr. Breynton at St. Paul's, and after the latter went to England in 1785, he and Mr. Weeks divided the duty between them. In 1789, Dr. Byles went to St. John, New Brunswick, where he became rector of Trinity Church, and chaplain of the Province. See the report of the S. P. G. for 1791, in which year Trinity Church was opened. At a vestry meeting of Trinity Church, December

8, 1791, it was resolved, "that the old Church be sold, price £200. The bell, organ, and King's Coat of Arms be removed to Trinity Church." These royal arms were probably originally on the walls of the council chamber of the Town House in Boston, whence they were taken by some of the Loyalists, when they left that city for St. John. In the council chamber they probably hung between the portraits of King Charles II. and King James II., "in a splendid golden frame."

Dr. Byles was a learned and able, and high-spirited man. He died at St. John, March 12, 1814, in his eightieth year. His daughter Anna was married at St. John, August 22, 1799, to Thomas Desbrisay, Lieutenant-Colonel of Artillery. His daughter Rebecca, born in New London, in 1762, was married to Dr. William James Almon, of Halifax, surgeon to the Ordnance and Artillery, and died there in 1853. His daughter Elizabeth was married to William Scovil of St. John, and died in 1808, aged forty-one. His son Belcher died in England in 1815, aged thirty-five. His son Mather died at Grenada, in 1803, aged thirty.

Henry Caner, D.D.

Henry Caner, D.D., a son of Henry and Abigail Caner, was born probably in New Haven, Conn., in 1700, and graduated at Yale College in 1724. In 1727, he went to England for ordination, and was appointed by the S. P. G., missionary at Fairfield, Conn. He also preached at Norwalk. November 27, 1746, the Reverend Roger Price of King's Chapel, Boston, resigned the rectorship of that parish, and Mr. Caner was called in his place. He was a popular preacher and very highly esteemed in Boston. In March, 1776, he left with the British troops for Halifax where, for a time, he had to accept the hospitality of the Reverend Dr. Breynton. Soon after, he sailed for England, and again in 1776 or '77 returned to America as a missionary of the S. P. G. to Bristol, Rhode Island, where he labored until the close of the war. He spent his late years in England and died in Long Ashton, in 1792, aged ninety-two.

Reverend Richard Samuel Clarke, M.A.

Reverend Richard Samuel Clarke was the fifth son of Samuel Clarke of West Haven, Conn., where he was born in 1737. He was graduated at Yale College in 1762, and the same year received the degree of M.A. from Kings College. He was lay reader in Salem, New York, for some time until he went to England for orders in 1766. His license from the Bishop of London "to preach in the Plantations" is dated February 25, 1767. After ordination he was appointed missionary to New Milford, Connecticut, where he stayed until 1786, when he went to New Brunswick, and settled at Gagetown. After twenty-five years there, he removed to St. Stephen, of which he was the first minister and where he died, October 6, 1824. The tablet above his grave states that he was minister at New Milford, Conn., nineteen years, of Gagetown, New Brunswick, twenty-five years, and of St. Stephen, thirteen years. He was "the oldest missionary in the present British colonies." His wife, Rebecca, died at St. Stephen, May 7, 1816, aged sixty-nine. His only surviving daughter, Mary Anne, died unmarried in Gagetown, in February, 1844, aged seventy-three.

Reverend William Clarke, M.A.

Reverend William Clarke was a son of the Reverend Peter Clarke of Danvers, Massachusetts, and was graduated at Harvard College in 1759. After ordination in England, he became rector of St. Paul's Church, Dedham. There he lived until 1777, when he was sentenced to be confined on board a ship because he refused to acknowledge the independency of America, which he says, "was contrary to the sentiments I had of my duty to my King, my country, and my God." After being released, he went first to Rhode Island, then to New York, then to Ireland, then to England; and in 1786, to Halifax, Nova Scotia, whence he soon removed to Digby. He finally returned to the United States and died in Quincy, Mass., in 1815. He married Mrs. Dunbar, a delicate young widow, who, Reverend Mr. Bailey wrote, was "as unable to rough it as himself."

Reverend Samuel Cooke, D.D.

Reverend Samuel Cooke was educated at Cambridge, England, and came to America as missionary of the S. P. G., probably as early as 1749. In 1765, he had charge of the churches in Shrewsbury, Freehold, and Middletown. The Revolution scattered his congregations and he became chaplain to the Guards, and in 1774 went to England, where in 1785 he received an appointment as one of the first missionaries to New Brunswick. August 18th, he landed at Halifax, where he received a hearty welcome from Governor Parr. September 2, 1785, he reached St. John, where he at once began his pastoral work, not limiting himself, however, to that settlement, but making missionary tours to other parts of the province. In 1785, he settled at Fredericton, where he was the first minister, and in 1790, was appointed commissary to the bishop of Nova Scotia. On the night of May 23, 1795, a dark and windy night, with his son he was crossing the St. John River, near Fredericton, in a birch canoe, when a sudden squall upset the canoe and both father and son were drowned. Mr. Cooke is justly styled the "father of the Church in New Brunswick." Bishop Inglis, writing of him to the S. P. G., said: "Never was a minister of the Gospel more beloved and esteemed, or more universally lamented in his death." Inscriptions to both father and son are to be seen on the walls of St. Ann's (Christ) Church, Fredericton. Dr. Cooke's wife was a Miss Kearney, of Amboy, New Jersey. He had at least five daughters, of whom one, Lydia, the fifth, died at Fredericton in 1846, aged seventy-six. His daughter Isabella, "the last survivor of his family," widow of Colonel Harris William Hales, died at Fredericton in 1848.

Reverend Nathaniel Fisher, M.A.

Reverend Nathaniel Fisher was born in Dedham, Mass., July 8, 1742. His father was a farmer of that place, and one of his sisters was the mother of Fisher Ames. Mr. Fisher was graduated at Harvard College in 1763. For some years he was in the service of the S. P. G., as schoolmaster at Granville. May 13, 1777, he was recommended to the Society "as a man of learning and good sense, of unexceptionable character, and worthy of being admitted to holy orders, as an assistant to the Rev. Mr. Wood of Annapolis." He crossed the Atlantic, was ordained by Bishop Lowth, and by him licensed as Mr. Wood's assistant. Early in 1778, the year of Mr. Wood's death, he arrived in Nova Scotia, and although the Rev.

Joshua Wingate Weeks was appointed to the church at Annapolis and Granville, he assumed the charge which he continued to hold till the close of 1781. He then returned to New England, and February 24, 1782, entered on his duties as rector of St. Peter's Church, Salem. There he remained until his death, on Sunday, December 20, 1812. He was buried in Salem. His wife was Silence Baker, of Dedham, by whom he had two sons and daughter. One of his sisters was the mother of Fisher Ames.

REVEREND BERNARD MICHAEL HOUSEAL.

Reverend Bernard Michael Houseal was senior pastor of the Lutheran Church in New York City, and in 1776, was one of the addressers of Lord Howe. From Nova Scotia he went to England in 1786, and, receiving Holy Orders, came back to Halifax as missionary to the Germans in that city. The report of the S. P. G. for 1786 calls him "a worthy man and a great sufferer by the late troubles." He died in Halifax, March 9, 1799.

REVEREND JOHN RUTGERS MARSHALL, M.A.

Reverend John Rutgers Marshall, M.A., was a graduate of King's College, New York, of

1770. In the convention of clergymen and laymen that met in New York, October 6, and 7, 1784, he was a deputy from Connecticut. Bishop Perry, in his "History of the American Episcopal Church," Vol. II., p. 27, describing this convention says: "Of this gentleman we know but little. His name occurs nowhere else on our journals or published records." In the record of him found in Nova Scotia history, Mr. Marshall's first name is not given, but there can be little doubt that it is this clergyman who is meant.

REVEREND JONATHAN ODELL, M.D.

Reverend Jonathan Odell was born at Newark, New Jersey, September 25, 1737, was an M.A. of Nassau Hall, was educated for the medical profession, and served as surgeon in the British army. He left the army while it was stationed in the West Indies, went to England and prepared for Holy Orders, and was ordained deacon in the Chapel Royal, St. James Palace, Westminster, by the Rt. Rev. Dr. Terrick, Bishop of London, December 21, 1766, and priest in January 1767. He was immediately appointed by the S. P. G. to succeed

Rev. Colin Campbell as missionary at Burlington, N. J., at which place he arrived July 25, 1767. Next day he was inducted into the pastorate of St. Ann's (now St. Mary's) Church by His Excellency, William Franklin, Esq., governor of the Province of New Jersey. May 6, 1772, he married Anne de Cou, and before leaving New Jersey had at least two children born, Mary, born March 19, 1773, and William Franklin, born October 19, 1774. Dr. Odell was devoted to the interests of his mission, but found it difficult to live on his salary, and so for a time practised medicine. In 1775, he was charged with writing letters to England, and was examined by the Provincial Congress of New Jersey, and by the Committee of Safety of Pennsylvania; and a year later was ordered to confine himself on parole, on the east side of the Delaware, within a circle of eight miles from the court house in Burlington. Later he was chaplain to a Loyalist corps. Arnold wrote a letter to André, August 30, 1780, "to be left at the Reverend Mr. Odell's, New York," a copy of which may be found in Sparks' "Washington." In the spring of 1782, standards were presented to the king's American

Dragoons, with imposing ceremonies, when the Rev. Dr. Odell made an address in the presence of a large number of distinguished officers of the British army and navy, including Prince William Henry, afterwards King William IV., who was at that time in New York as a midshipman in the fleet of Admiral Digby. When Sir Guy Carleton left New York, November 5, 1783, Dr. Odell accompanied him to England. Later he came to Nova Scotia, and when the new province of New Brunswick was formed, was appointed provincial secretary, register, and clerk of the council. He died in 1818. His daughter Lucy Anne, wife of Lieutenant-Colonel Rudyerd, of the Royal Engineers, died at Halifax in 1829. His son William Franklin, who was his successor as secretary, holding the office for thirty-two years, died at Fredericton, in 1844, aged seventy. Mary, his eldest daughter, died at Maugerville, New Brunswick, in 1848. Mrs. Odell died at Fredericton in 1825, aged eighty-five. Dr. Odell and Mr. Stansbury are called by Sabine "the two most important loyal versifiers of their time." "As a political satirist," says Winthrop Sargent, in his collections of the

"Loyalist Poetry of the Revolution," p. 202, "Dr. Odell is entitled to high rank. In fertility of conception, and vigor and ease of expression, many passages in his poems will compare favorably with those of Churchill and Canning."

REVEREND GEORGE PANTON, M.A.

Reverend George Panton was born in America, but was educated at the University of Aberdeen, from which he received the degree of M.A. In 1774, King's College, New York, also conferred on him the honorary degree of M.A. He was probably ordained in 1773. He was first, missionary at Trenton, N. J.; afterwards, at Philipsburg (Yonkers), New York, where he stayed until 1782. He then went to Nova Scotia, the Society continuing him a salary of £30 a year until he was again, in 1785, settled at Yarmouth and places adjacent. In 1786, he went to England, where he died.

REVEREND JOHN HAMILTON ROWLAND, D.D.

Reverend John Hamilton Rowland was a Pennsylvania clergyman. Before 1786 he removed to Shelburne, Nova Scotia, and became rector of St. Patrick's Church. In 1791, the parish of St. Patrick's was united to St. George's and Mr. Rowland made sole rector. He died in 1795 in his forty-fourth year and was succeeded in the rectorship by his son, Reverend Thomas Bolby Rowland. He is described as a learned man and a good preacher.

Reverend James Sayre, M.A.

Reverend James Sayre was educated to the law and admitted to practice in New York in 1771. In 1774, King's College gave him the degree of M.A., and shortly before the Revolution, he entered the ministry. During the war he became chaplain to one of De Lancey's battalions, but "impelled by distress, severity of treatment, and by.duty," he resigned this post in 1777. From 1778 to 1783, he was rector of the Episcopal church in Brooklyn, New York. In the latter year, he became a grantee of St. John, New Brunswick, where he lived for a short time. He soon returned, however, to the United States and from 1786 to 1788 was rector at Newport, Rhode Island. He died at Fairfield, Connecticut, in 1798, aged fifty-three.

Reverend John Sayre.

Reverend John Sayre was S. P. G. missionary at Fairfield, Conn., for several years before the Revolution. His well-known attachment to the crown compelled him, after Tryon burned the town, to fly from the colony. He went from Fairfield to Flushing, Long Island, but in 1781 was in New York. In 1783, he was one of the fifty-five petitioners for grants of land in Nova Scotia. In October of the same year he went to St. John, New Brunswick, became a grantee of that city, and was appointed by Lord Dorchester one of the agents of Government to locate the lands granted to the Loyalists in New Brunswick. In St. John he received what was known as lot 36, Dock Street. He soon moved to Maugerville on the river St. John, but died August 5, 1784, in his forty-eighth year. His daughter Esther was married to Christopher Robinson, who was appointed Deputy Surveyor of Crown Lands in Upper Canada. They were the parents of Sir Beverley Robinson, Chief Justice of Ontario, and grand-parents of Honorable John Beverley Robinson, at one time Lieutenant-Governor of Ontario. Reverend John Sayre was a brother of Reverend James Sayre.

REVEREND JAMES SCOVIL, M.A.

Reverend James Scovil, son of Lieut. William Scovil, was born at Waterbury, Connecticut, in 1733, and graduated at Yale College in 1757. In 1759 he was S. P. G. missionary in his native town, soon afterward extending his labors to New Cambridge and Northbury. During the Revolution, though his sympathies were with the crown "he behaved with so much prudence and moderation, that he escaped everything like personal indignity." At the close of the war, the Venerable Society withdrawing its support from the clergymen who remained in the United States, but offering an increase of salary to those who would remove to the loyal provinces, Mr. Scovil reluctantly left his charge, and in May, 1786, went to New Brunswick, where he became missionary at Kingston. His son, Reverend Elias Scovil, succeeded him in the rectorship of the Kingston Church, and held this position for many years. Reverend James Scovil died at Kingston, December 19, 1808, and his widow in 1832, aged ninety years. Reverend Elias Scovil, one of the oldest missionaries of the S. P. G., died at Kingston in 1841, at the age of seventy.

REVEREND EPENETUS TOWNSEND, M.A.

Reverend Epenetus Townsend was graduated at King's College, New York, in 1759, and about 1767 went to England for Orders. He returned in 1768 and entered on his duties at North Salem, New York. In 1776 he was sent to the Whig Committee, but was dismissed. Three weeks after the Declaration of Independence, says Sabine, he abandoned his pulpit, and in October was a prisoner at Fishkill. In March, 1777, he was removed to Long Island, and shortly afterwards embarked with his family for Nova Scotia. The vessel unfortunately foundered and every one on board perished.

REVEREND ROGER VIETS, M.A.

Reverend Roger Viets, son of John and Lois (Phelps) Viets was born in Simsbury, Conn., in 1737. He was uncle to the Right Reverend Bishop Griswold. He entered Yale College at the early age of thirteen and graduated in 1758.

The parents of Mr. Viets were zealous Presbyterians, but his own studies led him to embrace the doctrines of the Episcopal church. Overcoming the opposition of his friends, he went to England, was ordained, and returned to become S. P. G. missionary in his native town. For the crime of giving food to some Loyalists, who came to his house at midnight, he was sentenced to pay a fine of £20 and to be imprisoned for one year in Hartford jail. In 1786 he became rector of the church in Digby, Nova Scotia. He died at Digby in 1811, after a ministry there of twenty-four years.

Reverend William Walter, D.D.

Reverend William Walter, D.D., born October 7, 1737, was the eldest son of the Reverend Nathaniel Walter, pastor of the Second Church in Roxbury, Mass., who died in 1776. He was graduated at Harvard College in 1756. One of his sisters was married to Sir Robert Hasilrigge, Bart., and another to the Reverend Mather Byles, D.D., Junior. In 1764, in company with Abraham Jarvis, afterward bishop of Connecticut, and others, he went to England for ordination, and on his return, July 22, 1764, was installed rector of Trinity Church, Boston. September 30, 1766, he married Lydia, daughter of the Honorable Benjamin Lynde, Junior, of Salem, who bore him seven children. His grandson Lynde Minshall Walter was the founder and first editor of the *Boston Evening Transcript.* In March, 1776, Dr. Walter resigned his rectorship and left with the British troops for Halifax. His youngest daughter, Harriet Tynge, was born in Shelburne, May 16, 1776. Although his family remained in Nova Scotia, he himself returned with General Howe and the fleet to New York, where he was on the 31st of October, 1776. Later, in August, 1783, he went back to Nova Scotia and was settled at Shelburne. He perhaps came to Shelburne with the New York people who settled there in 1783. In 1791, he returned to Boston, where he purchased a house in Charter Street, built by Sir William Phipps, and destroyed in 1837. May 28, 1792, he became rector of Christ Church, Boston, which office he held until December 5, 1800. He was "a remarkably handsome man, tall and well-proportioned. When in the street he always wore a long blue cloth cloak over his cassock and gown; a full-bottomed wig, dressed and powdered; a three-cornered hat; knee breeches of fine black cloth, with black silk hose; and square-quartered shoes, with silver buckles. His countenance was always serene; his temper always cheerful."

REVEREND JOSHUA WINGATE WEEKS, M.A.

Reverend Joshua Wingate Weeks was the eldest child of Colonel John and Mrs. Martha Weeks. He was born at Hampton, New Hampshire (the date of his birth is not known), and graduated at Harvard College in 1758. He married Sarah Treadwell, of Ipswich, Mass., was ordained in England in 1761, and in 1762 became rector of St. Michael's Church, Marblehead, Massachusetts. In 1775, he was driven from that place by "the political commotions of the time," and took refuge with the Rev. Jacob Bailey, his brother-in-law, at Pownalboro, Me. He returned to Massachusetts, however, and in 1778 asked permission to leave the country. His petition was rejected, but he did leave, and for a time was in England, whence he came to Nova Scotia in 1779, three weeks after Mr.

Bailey arrived. The Reverend Thomas Wood having died, December 14, 1778, Mr. Weeks was appointed missionary to Annapolis in his place, but instead of going there he remained in Halifax for a few months, and then sailed for New York, the Rev. Nathaniel Fisher, afterward of St. Peter's Church, Salem, doing duty at Annapolis instead. In November, 1779, Mrs. Weeks and her eight children came to Halifax, and there, in the spring of 1780, Mr. Weeks joined them. He seems to have preferred staying at Halifax to going to his mission, and for a time was a garrison chaplain, and assistant to Dr. Breynton, the rector of St. Paul's. Dr. Mather Byles was in Halifax at this time, and was likewise a garrison chaplain. Dr. George Hill, the historian of St. Paul's Church, thinks that Dr. Byles may have been senior, Mr. Weeks junior chaplain. For a time Mr. Weeks drew from the S. P. G. seventy pounds a year, which was half the salary apportioned for the Annapolis mission, but the Society, not pleased with his remaining away from his work, in 1780 appointed the Rev. Jacob Bailey to the mission. In 1785, the Rev. Dr. Breynton went to England, and until his successor, Mr. Stanser, was inducted into the rectorship in 1791, and indeed somewhat longer, Mr. Weeks had either sole or partial charge of St. Paul's parish. After that he officiated, it is said, at Preston and Guysborough, and "could have been settled at Digby." Like most of the other Loyalist clergy who came to Nova Scotia, he was poor, sometimes in actual distress; he died in Nova Scotia in 1804, and has still descendants in the province. One of his daughters was married, October 5, 1789, to the Rev. William Twining, missionary at Rawdon, and became the mother of the Rev. John Thomas Twining, so often affectionately alluded to in the life of Captain Hedley Vicars.

Reverend Isaac Wilkins, S.T.D.

Reverend Isaac Wilkins, son of Martin Wilkins, a rich planter of Jamaica, West Indies, of a Welsh family, was born in Jamaica in 1741 and was sent to New York to be educated. In 1756, he entered King's College (Columbia), graduated in 1760, and in 1763, received the degree of M.A. He prepared for the ministry, but did not take orders. He married, November 7, 1762, Isabella, daughter of the

Honorable Lewis Morris, and sister of Lewis and Gouverneur Morris[1] (born February 14, 1748), and settled at "Castle Hill," Westchester, from which county he was returned to the assembly, where he soon became a leader and acquired great personal influence. He was a man of profound convictions and early in the Revolution his zeal for the British cause made him peculiarly obnoxious to the Whigs. He wrote and spoke strongly, and to some of his political essays Hamilton, also born in the West Indies, replied. In 1775 he went to England, where he stayed a year, and there is not wanting evidence that he tried hard to bring about an amicable settlement of the American troubles. Leaving England, he returned to Long Island, and then came to Shelburne, Nova Scotia, where, and at Lunenburg, he lived until about 1798, when he went back to

---

[1] The Morris family was singularly divided in the Revolution. Mrs. Wilkins' mother espoused the royal side, and remained within the British lines, her brother Lewis was a signer of the Declaration of Independence, her brother Gouverneur was a distinguished Whig, and her brother Staats was an officer in the royal service, and later became a member of parliament and a lieutenant-general. Three of the sons of Lewis served in the Whig army.

Westchester. In that year he was ordained deacon, and in 1799, priest, by Bishop Provoost, and became rector of St. Peter's, Westchester, giving also part of his time to St. Paul's, Eastchester. He retained the rectorship of St. Peter's until he died, February 5, 1830. He was made S.T.D. by Columbia College in 1811, and for many years was the oldest surviving alumnus. He had twelve children, one of whom, Lewis Morris, was a member of the House of Assembly of Nova Scotia, speaker of that body, and a judge of the supreme court. He died at Windsor, late in 1847, or early in 1848. His son Lewis Morris was also a judge of the supreme court. In Nova Scotia Mr. Wilkins was much in public life. Gouverneur Morris Wilkins writes: "He had a clear voice, but with that refined and pleasing tone which often sorts with generous blood." His epitaph in St. Peter's Church, written by himself, is as follows:

SACRED
To the memory of
The Reverend ISAAC WILKINS, D.D.,
who, for thirty-one years, was the
diligent and faithful minister
of this parish,
placed here, as he believed, by his Redeemer.

He remained satisfied with the
pittance allowed him and rejoicing that even in that
he was no burden to his
parishioners;
nor ever wished, nor ever went forth
to seek a better living.

REVEREND JOHN WISWELL, M.A.

Reverend John Wiswell was the son of John Wiswell. He was born in Boston, April 3, 1731, and graduated at Harvard College in 1749. As early as 1753, he began a school at Falmouth, Maine, and in 1756 was ordained pastor of the Congregational church in New Casco. In 1764, he changed his religious views, and having accepted a call from an Episcopal church, then forming in Falmouth, went to England for ordination, returning in May, 1765. July, 1766, his flock consisted of seventy families, besides, as he wrote at the time, "a considerable number of strangers." The S. P. G. gave twenty pounds towards his salary, and his people made up the rest. In 1775, when Falmouth was burned by Mowatt, St. Paul's Church, in which he officiated, was burned, and he himself was seized, and carried before the Whig Committee a prisoner. He was soon released, however, and "yielding to circumstances," left the town. He went first to England, where, in 1781, he was a curate at Oxford. In 1782, he came to Nova Scotia, having been appointed missionary for Cornwallis, Horton, and Wilmot. He died at Wilmot, December 2, 1812, aged eighty-one. The inscription on his tombstone in Wilmot is as follows:

SACRED
To the memory of
The Reverend JOHN WISWELL, A.M.,
who was born in Boston, U. S., 3rd
April, 1731, ordained by the
Bishop of London, 1764.
He left his native land in 1775, in consequence
of the Revolutionary struggle, and was
appointed rector of the parish
of Wilmot in 1789, where
he continued until his
death, 2nd Dec.,
1812.
He was the first clergyman of any
denomination who settled in
this place.

He has descendants still in Nova Scotia. One of his sons was the Hon. Peleg Wiswell, who was appointed an "Associate Circuit Judge," March 30, 1816, and died at Annapolis in 1836, aged seventy-four.

CHAPTER XI.

KING'S COLLEGE.

THE interest in education taken by the Church of England, wherever she has planted herself, is too well known to need comment here. The noble work of the Society for the Propagation of the Gospel, from the first, included the establishment of schools and school-masters in all the distant fields to which its missionaries were sent. In the Society's report presented in 1750, the Lords of Trade are said to have lately declared their intention of setting apart in each of the new townships to be formed in Nova Scotia, four hundred acres of land for a church, and two hundred for a school, these grants to be further increased by grants of two hundred acres to every clergyman as his own private property, and one hundred to every school-master, with thirty acres over for each person belonging to their respective families, these lands to be subject to no quit rent.¹ Their lordships, therefore, recommend to the Society to name schoolmasters as well as ministers to be sent over to the new colony. At first, as we have seen, but one school-master was sent, a Mr. Edward Halhead, whose name does not appear in the Society's reports after 1752. In the report of 1755, two school-masters are mentioned, Mr. Hobley, school-master to the English, and Mr. Bailly, school-master to the French. In the report of 1757, Mr. Hobley's name is supplanted by that of Mr. Ralph Sharrock, "a well-behaved, pious soldier," Mr. Hobley having

---

¹ In 1785 the governor sent to the S.P.G. a list of thirty-one townships where lands had been set apart, that the Society might know where to send missionaries and school-masters. The school lands of Nova Scotia have at various times been the subject of much dispute in the provincial legislature and in the different counties where they are located. In 1761, the grants of glebe land were increased, in some townships, to 600 acres, and of school land to 400 acres, "making together two shares for the use of the church and school forever." In 1787, all the school lands were vested either in rectors and wardens, or in the bishop and two other trustees. But in 1838 and 1839, a strong effort was made legally to vest these lands in trustees for the purpose of *general education*. This effort failed, but there seems to have been in some places a quiet renunciation by the Church of such revenues as came from school lands, in favor of the public schools. The public school system of Nova Scotia, it is well known, is most thorough and efficient.

been dismissed by Dr. Breynton for negligence in the performance of his duties. When Bishop Inglis reached his diocese in 1787, he found in Nova Scotia, schools with school-masters at Annapolis, Granville, Lunenburg, Wilmot, Cornwallis, Digby, and undoubtedly Shelburne and Halifax, where the schools must have been by this time self-supporting; in New Brunswick, he found schools at St. John, Carleton, St. Andrews, and probably Fredericton, Maugerville, and Kingston.

With the formation of the diocese a new era in education dawned for the province. Five of the eighteen clergymen who met in New York in March, 1783, to formulate a plan for the establishment of a see in Nova Scotia, on the 18th of October of that year, re-assembled to perfect a plan, which early in March had also been outlined, for a "Religious and Literary Institution for the Province of Nova Scotia."[1] It would be unfair, however, to the early government of Nova Scotia, to imagine that the men who composed it, and the governors who

---

[1] This plan is printed in the Reports of the Nova Scotia Historical Society, vol. vi., p. 125. It is dated March 8, 1783.

presided over the colony, had themselves never felt the necessity for a Church college. In 1768, a plan for a school was submitted by the governor and council to the Board of Trade, but this body felt that money for such an object should come from within the colony rather than from England, and so passed the Nova Scotia petition by. The next year the provincial government laid their plan before the S. P. G., mentioning Windsor as the most suitable place for a school, but the Venerable Society was short of funds and had to refuse the request for aid. When Bishop Inglis entered on his episcopate in 1787, the school had not been formed, and he soon wrote: "One great object of my appointment is to ordain candidates for holy orders, to supply vacant churches with clergymen, who cannot be supplied from Europe. But if there is no seminary we cannot expect any to be duly educated and qualified for orders; and consequently none can be ordained, so that, in fact, the want of a seminary will totally defeat, in this respect, one principal object which government had in view, by appointing a bishop, as well as the benefits thereby intended for the Church of England."

His first letter to the Archbishop of Canterbury after his consecration, dated at Halifax, December 26, 1787, contains this information: "The Assembly of this province met the latter end of October; some of the principal members of which were my old friends. To these I communicated my wishes respecting a public grammar school, and urged the absolute necessity of the legislature's interference and support for the purpose. These friends perfectly concurred in opinon with me, and promised their warmest support. I afterward spoke to several other leading members of the assembly on the subject; and while matters were in this state, the packet arrived with the governor's instructions relative to a bishop. I immediately requested Governor Parr to lay the King's instruction relative to schools before the council and assembly, which he did, and soon after, the assembly voted the sum of £400, to be appropriated to the use of an academy, in the manner which your grace will see directed in the proceedings of the assembly which accompany this letter."

The "proceedings" which accompanied this letter were a resolution of the assembly passed in November, 1787, that a seminary should be established in some suitable place, with four hundred pounds a year to pay teachers' salaries; the head master of the school, who should be a clergyman of the Established Church, to receive two hundred pounds sterling, and a professor of mathematics and natural philosophy to receive one hundred. The men presenting this resolution express themselves as fearful that if the Nova Scotia youth are sent to the United States for instruction, they will lose their attachment to their native land, and imbibe principles unfriendly to the British constitution. They declare Nova Scotia in point of "situation, climate, salubrity of air, and fertility of soil, inferior to no country and superior to most," and recommend Windsor as the best place for the proposed school. The governing body of this school, it is recommended, shall consist of the lieutenant-governor, the bishop, the chief justice, the president of the council, and the speaker of the house of assembly.

The school was soon established, and Mr. Archibald Peane Inglis, a nephew of the bishop, appointed its "president," or principal. It was formally opened by Bishop Inglis, November 1, 1788, seventeen students being in attendance. The first school-house was the private residence of Mrs. Susanna Francklin, widow of the Honorable Michael Francklin, daughter of Joseph Boutineau of Boston, and granddaughter of Peter Faneuil of that city; the trustees of the school, Governor Parr, Bishop Inglis, Richard Bulkeley, Sampson Salter Blowers, and Richard John Uniacke, having leased the property from Mrs. Francklin and her son, James Boutineau Francklin, for a period of five years. In a short time Mr. Archibald Peane Inglis, who afterwards became a clergyman, was succeeded in the principalship by Mr. William Cochran, an Irish gentleman, born in county Tyrone, a graduate of Trinity College, Dublin, and sometime professor of Greek and Latin in King's College, New York. Desirous of taking orders "and finding that ordination in the United States would debar him from preferment under English authority," Mr. Cochran resolved to apply to the bishop of Nova Scotia. He resigned his professorship in King's College, New York, and came to Nova Scotia in October, 1788.[1] He

---

[1] "Kings College, Windsor," by H. Y. Hind, pp. 24, 25.

received the degree of S. T. D. from Trinity College, Dublin, in 1802, and died August 4, 1833.

In 1789, an act was passed by the legislature of Nova Scotia, entitled, "An Act for Founding, Establishing, and Maintaining a College in this Province," the opening clause of which is: "Whereas, *the permanent establishment and effectual support of a college at Windsor, may, by the blessing of God, become of the greatest public utility to this province, and to His Majesty's neighboring colonies: Be it therefore enacted by the Lieutenant-Governor, Council, and Assembly*, That a sum not exceeding four hundred and forty-four pounds eight shillings and ten pence half-penny, current money of Nova Scotia, equal to four hundred pounds, sterling money of Great Britain, shall be yearly, and every year, granted, allowed, and paid by, from, or out of such monies as may, from time to time, be collected and paid into the public treasury of this province from the duties imposed, or to be imposed, on brown and loaf, or refined sugars; and in case such duties are not sufficient to answer the said sum at the days and time of payment thereof, then by, from, or out of any other aids, supplies, or taxes not otherwise specially appropriated to other uses; which sum of four hundred and forty-four pounds eight shillings and ten pence half-penny, shall be drawn by warrant, under the hand and seal of the governor, lieutenant-governor, or commander-in-chief for the time being, on the provincial treasurer in the way usually practised in equal quarterly payments; the first quarter to commence the first of January, one thousand seven hundred and eighty-nine, and to be drawn for on the first of April, and so on from quarter to quarter as the same shall grow due, on the requisition of the governors of the said college, or the major part of them, as hereinafter appointed, for or toward the maintenance and support of the said college, and the payment of the salaries of the president and professors to be by them appointed."

This act likewise provided that a sum not exceeding five hundred pounds should be drawn from the public treasury for the purchase of property and the erection of buildings in Windsor, for the establishment of the college, and gave the governors power to elect a temporary president and professors. The president, it declared, should always be "a clergyman of the Church of England, duly qualified for that office." The college was opened in 1790, probably in the Francklin house, Mr. Cochran, who had lately been ordained, taking temporary charge on the first of June.

The buildings of King's College, begun in 1791, stand on a picturesque slope, a little out of the town of Windsor, not far from the Avon River. The main college hall is a fine old colonial wooden building, with a portico raised on high Doric pillars, a convocation hall, and a stone chapel, called the Hensley Memorial Chapel, near. On three sides extend the spacious grounds of the college, which comprise a noble estate of sixty-nine acres, purchased in 1790, and bounded by lands, which in old times were the properties of the rich land-owners and country gentlemen, who constituted the aristocratic society of Windsor. For the construction of the original buildings, the Imperial Government at first granted three thousand pounds, but this amount proving insufficient, in 1794 the governors asked for a grant of fifteen hundred pounds more. The college obtained its charter, May 12, 1802, the governors then named being Lieutenant-Governor Sir John Wentworth, Bart., Bishop Charles Inglis, Chief Justice Blowers, Alexander Croke, Judge of the Court of Vice-Admiralty, Richard John Uniacke, Speaker of the House and Attorney-General, and Benning Wentworth, Provincial Secretary, with four others to be elected, one of whom was to be the president of the college. The charter was accompanied by an imperial grant of a thousand pounds per annum, which was continued until 1834.[1]

The power of making statutes for the college corporation was vested in the board of governors, who met for that purpose shortly after the charter was received. At the meeting a committee of three was appointed to draft statutes, and report at some future day. The committee consisted of the bishop, Judge Alexander Croke, and Chief-Justice Blowers, who soon presented their report, which was

---

[1] In New Brunswick a college with a royal charter was founded in 1828, which for many years was sustained by an imperial grant, together with an appropriation from the local legislation. It was well endowed, but relinquishing its charter, lost its hold on the Church. This institution, known as the "University of New Brunswick," is situated at Fredericton.

adopted. These first statutes nearly crushed the infant college, and worked more mischief to the Church of England in Nova Scotia than anything else in her history has done. The grant of the provincial government, in 1797, was for a Church school, but its wider aim was to promote higher education among all denominations in the province. The committee appointed to frame statues, were instructed to take the statutes of Oxford University as their model, and notwithstanding the different conditions existing in Nova Scotia, where either the Roman Catholics, the Presbyterians, or the Baptists, outnumbered the Church, one of the statutes presented, required from all matriculants, subscription to the thirty-nine articles. To this requirement Bishop Inglis, with rather more foresight and fairness of mind, strongly objected, but Chief Justice Blowers sided with Judge Croke who had been allowed to draw up the paper, and the latter carried them through. From Judge Croke's high-handed legislation, the bishop appealed to the Archbishop of Canterbury, who was the patron of the college, and eventually a new code was adopted, but unluckily, this time the bishop was at fault, for instead of at once abolishing all religious tests, in a college for a new, mixed colony, he modified the obnoxious statute only so far as to permit persons to study at King's without subscription to the articles, still precluding them from taking degrees. To this unjust and foolish restriction was added the still more stupid and objectionable law that no student at King's should "frequent the Romish mass or the meeting houses of Presbyterians, Baptists, or Methodists, or the coventicles or places of worship of any other dissenters from the Church of England, or where divine service should not be performed according to the liturgy of the Church of England, or be present at any seditious or rebellious meetings." The effect of such a statute as this on the college was exactly what might have been foreseen. The prospect of a college in the province was welcomed by educated persons of every shade of belief, but the adoption of such a law as this, of course, shut the doors of King's College in the faces of all youths desiring an education, not nominally members of the Church of England, and a final wrong was done when in 1818, the Archbishop of Canterbury, who had, it must be confessed, in the beginning been in favor of allowing all persons without distinction of sect to study at King's College, provided that without subscription to the thirty-nine articles, none should take degrees, peremptorily refused his sanction to the urgent appeal of Lord Dalhousie, the governor of the province, and others, that subscription to the articles, even for degrees, should henceforth be discontinued. Under the weight of this statute, the college groaned until 1830, when at last, except in the cases of professors and fellows, subscription to the articles was formally abolished. The mischief done by it in alienating large numbers of intelligent people in the province from the Church of England, in dividing educational forces, and producing bitter local prejudices, can never be estimated. Somewhere in the early records of the college is an accidental statement of what no doubt, apart from religious narrowness, was the strongest reason in the minds of many persons in England and in Nova Scotia for sacredly guarding the college from the intrusion of non-subscribers to the thirty-nine articles. It is there said to be believed "that in exact proportion to the influence of the established religion will be the immovable loyalty of the inhabitants of the province." In 1851, the provincial legislature finally withdrew its annual grant of four hundred pounds sterling to the college, thus leaving it as it still is, under the direct patronage and protection of the Archbishop of Canterbury, and largely dependent for support upon the alumni and the members of the Church throughout the province. From 1790 to 1803, before the charter was obtained, King's College had in all two hundred graduates: from 1803 to 1810, twenty-one; from 1810 to 1820, fifty-one; from 1820 to 1830, sixty-nine; and from 1830 to 1840, forty-eight. Of this number, fifty-four, in all, became clergymen.

The following are some of the more distinguished pre-charter students of this oldest colonial college of the British empire, and the chief facts of their lives:

Major-General James Robertson Arnold, son of the notorious Benedict Arnold, entered the British army in 1798, and was colonel commanding the engineers at Halifax in 1825 and '26. In 1801, he served in the Egyptian campaign, and was at the taking of Alexandria and Cairo. Later, he served also in the West Indies, was severely wounded in leading the storming party at Fort Leydon, and was presented with a sword of honor from the committee of the patriotic fund. He died in England.

Colonel de Lancey Barclay, A.D.C. to Prince Frederick, Duke of York and Albany, was the son of Thomas Barclay, and grandson of Dr. Henry Barclay, Rector of Trinity Church, New York. He died in 1826, having repeatedly distinguished himself, especially at Waterloo, where he was an officer under the Duke of Wellington.

Sir James Cochran, Chief Justice of Gibraltar, was a son of the Honorable Thomas Cochran, M.L.C. His mother was a daughter of Mr. William Allen, of Cumberland. He graduated at King's, and was admitted to the bar of the province, July 21, 1817, but never practised. In 1814, he was appointed secretary and treasurer of the governors of the college, the duties of which office he performed until 1818, when he was succeeded by his friend, James Walton Nutting. In 1829 he was admitted to the English bar, and the following year received the appointment of attorney-general of Gibraltar. In 1841, he became chief justice and was knighted. Sir James married, in 1829, Theresa, daughter of Colonel William Haley, who died in 1873. He died in England June 24, 1866, several children surviving him. For many years he corresponded regularly with his old college friend, Dr. James C. Cochran, who was not related to him.

General William Cochran was a brother of Sir James. He entered the army in 1805, and became lieutenant-colonel in 1824. The same year he was appointed inspecting field officer of militia in Nova Scotia. On his return to England he received the appointment of deputy military secretary at Horse Guards. Colonel Cochran served in the Spanish campaign under Wellington, and afterwards in America. He died in England at an advanced age. One of his sisters was the wife of Bishop John Inglis, another was Isabella, wife of Dean Ramsay, of Edinburgh, a half-sister was the wife of Commodore Sir Dennis George, Bart., and mother of Sir Rupert Dennis George, for many years provincial secretary at Halifax.

The Honorable Henry H. Cogswell was admitted to the bar of Nova Scotia at a very early period, served in the house of assembly for the town of Halifax, and was afterward appointed a member of Her Majesty's council. He was for many years president of the Halifax Banking Company, and registrar of the court of chancery, which office he resigned on his appointment to the council. In 1847, his alma mater conferred on him the degree of D.C.L. His sons James C. Cogswell, Henry Ellis Cogswell, Dr. Charles Cogswell, and Rev. William Cogswell, like their father, were all graduates of King's college.

Colonel Sir William F. de Lancey, K.C.B., a son of Stephen de Lancey of New York, the noted Loyalist, went with his father to Nova Scotia at the close of the Revolution. He entered the British army, and at Waterloo, where he died, was deputy quartermaster-general of the troops and an intimate friend of the Duke of Wellington. Stephen de Lancey, his father, was Chief Justice of the Bahama Islands, and after that Governor of Tobago. Susan de Lancey, a daughter of Sir William, was the wife of Sir Hudson Lowe, the governor of St. Helena during Napoleon's captivity there.

Sir William de Lancey was buried in the old cemetery at Brussels, where his grave was to be seen in 1888. His body has since then been removed to the new cemetery.

The Honorable Charles R. Fairbanks was admitted to the bar of Nova Scotia in 1810, and was member for Halifax for several years. On the death of Judge S. G. W. Archibald, he became judge of the court of vice-admiralty and master of the rolls.

Lieutenant-Colonel William Hulme entered the army soon after leaving college. He was regimental major and brevet lieutenant-colonel of the 96th regiment, which was quartered at Halifax in 1830. He, later, served in India.

Judge Richard John Uniacke was admitted to the bar of Nova Scotia in 1810. Before the annexation of Cape Breton to Nova Scotia, he was attorney-general of that island, after which he represented Cape Breton in the provincial assembly from 1820 until 1830. In the latter year he was elevated to the bench of the Supreme court. Judge Uniacke, who was remarkable " for his handsome person and amiable disposition," belonged to a family than which none in Nova Scotia stood higher for ability and integrity. He died at the early age of forty-eight, his life having been shortened by the shock he received from the death of Mr. Bowie, his antagonist in a duel to which he had been challenged. This challenge was caused by some remarks made by Mr. Uniacke in charging a jury.

Other pre-charter students of King's were: Rev. James Bissett, B. de St. Croix, Rev. Benjamin G. Gray, Bishop John Inglis, Rev. Cyrus Perkins, Rev. Thomas Bolby Rowland, the Venerable George O'Kill Stewart, Archdeacon of Upper Canada, Hon. Sir James Stewart, Kt., Attorney-General of Lower Canada, and Rev. Charles W. Weeks. Later distinguished graduates before 1820 were: Hon. W. B. Almon, A. Barclay, Rev. Hibbert Binney, Hon. A. W. Cochran, Rev. E. A. Crawley, Rev. J. W. D. Gray, Judge T. C. Haliburton, J. Lawson, Rev. G. McCawley, a President of King's college, Rev. J. T. T. Moody, James Walton Nutting, Rev. John Pryor, Rev. John Thomas Twining, Rev. R. F. Uniacke, Judge Lewis M. Wilkins, and Martin I. Wilkins. Nearly all these eminent men received from their alma mater, either the degree of D.C.L. or of D.D. Three of them, Messrs. Crawley, Nutting, and Pryor, in 1828, became Baptists, and were long leaders in the Baptist denomination. Of Mr. Nutting the late Dr. Thomas B. Akins writes: "James Walton Nutting was the son of John Nutting, a loyalist gentleman from the revolted provinces. He entered college in 1804 and took his B.A. in 1810, receiving the honorary degree of D.C.L. in 1868, being the oldest graduate of King's College then living. Mr. Nutting was admitted to the bar on October 23, 1810. He became secretary to the governors in 1818 on the resignation of Sir James Cochran. He held the office of prothonotary and clerk of the crown until his death in 1870. Mr. Nutting occupied a high social position in Halifax; his geniality of manner, philanthropy, and piety endearing him both to bar and bench, and to a large circle of friends. He was offered a seat in the legislative council during the administration of Sir Colin Campbell, which he declined, not wishing to enter into politics. He died at the age of eighty-three, universally respected."

Distinguished graduates of King's since 1820 have been: Henry Bliss, Hon. Wm. Blowers Bliss, R. Christie, Rev. J. H. Clinch, Rev. Wm. Cogswell, Sir Edward Cunard, Bart., Judge John Gray, Hon. Wm. Hill, Hon. Edw. James Jarvis, Chief Justice of Prince Edward Island, Hon. Neville Parker, Hon. Robert Parker, Rt. Rev. Thomas G. Suther, Bishop of Aberdeen, Hon. James B. Uniacke, Hon. R. F. Uniacke, and Major Augustus Welsford, 97th Regt., who was killed in the Crimea.

Undoubtedly the most distinguished person that ever studied at King's College was *General Sir John Eardley Wilmot Inglis*, K.C.B., who is known in history as the "Hero of Lucknow"—the man who saved India to the Br tish Empire. General Inglis, a son of Bishop John Inglis, was born in Halifax and matriculated at King's College in 1831. He did not graduate but entered the army in 1833, his first campaign being with the 32d Regiment in Canada during the rebellion of 1837, where he was present at the battles of St. Denis and St. Eustache. Though at that time but a subaltern in charge of a skirmishing party, which was covering the retreat from St. Denis, he called his men together, charged through the village under a brisk fire from the houses, and brought off two field pieces which had been left amid the snow by the retreating party. For this service he was mentioned in dispatches. He served in the Punjaub campaigns of 1848 and 1849, being present at the first and second operation before Mooltan, including the attack on the advanced trenches on the 12th of September; where, after the death of Lieutenant-Colonel Pattoun, he succeeded to the command of the right column of attack. He commanded the 32d at the action of Soorjkoond, and also at the storming and capture of the city and surrender of the fort and garrison of Channiote, and the battle of Goojerat, for which service he received the rank of lieutenant-colonel, with medal and clasps. Going to India the second time, he received the rank of full colonel, and being with his regiment at Lucknow, at the time of the Indian mutiny, on the death of the officer in command of the garrison, who was killed early in the attack on the residency, the command of the forces devolved on him, as the senior colonel then present. The terrible scenes which there occurred, and the heroic acts of the defenders of the city are matters of history.

After the defense of Lucknow, Colonel Inglis was rewarded with the rank of major-general and the Knighthood of the Bath, but the continued suffering which he had undergone in India, and the almost total loss of sleep, had shaken his constitution, originally strong and robust. Though appointed to lucrative and important military commands, his failing health soon necessitated his retirement from active service. He was then recommended by his physicians to take a course of treatment at the German baths. But all was in vain; and he died at the early age of forty-four.[1] His wife was Miss Thesiger, daughter of Lord Chelmsford, who accompanied him to India, and shared with him the terrors and sufferings of the siege. In 1858, King's College conferred on General Inglis the degree of D.C.L.

---

[1] This sketch of General Inglis is abridged from one published in a newspaper by the late Dr. Thomas B. Akins.

CHAPTER XII.

THE CHURCH'S GROWTH.

THE condition of affairs in the new diocese of Nova Scotia, when Bishop Charles Inglis came to it in 1787, was briefly as follows: In Nova Scotia proper there were twelve missionaries at work: Dr. Breynton in St. Paul's, Halifax, Mr. Houseal among the Germans in St. George's, Halifax, Mr. Bailey at Annapolis, Mr. Money at Lunenburg, Mr. Ellis at Windsor, Mr. Wiswell at Cornwallis and Horton, Mr. Eagleson in Cumberland, Mr. Viets at Digby, Mr. de la Roche at Guysborough, Mr. Shreve at Parrsborough, and Dr. Walter and Mr. Rowland at Shelburne. In New Brunswick, as we have already seen, there were six: Mr. Cooke at Fredericton, Dr. Byles at St. John, Mr. Beardsley at Maugerville, Mr. Scovil at Kingston, Mr. Andrews at St. Andrews, and Mr. Clarke at Gagetown. In Cape Breton there was one; Mr. Ranna (Réné) Cossit, who had been sent out from England by the S. P.

G., in 1765, with instructions "to repair with all convenient speed to Cape Breton," and who, establishing himself at Sydney, was the only missionary in the island for many years. In Prince Edward Island there was probably but one, Mr. Des Brisay, of Trinity College, Dublin, who in 1775 "was appointed by His Majesty, George III., rector of the parish of Charlotte."[1] After his first episcopal visitation, the bishop wrote the Society that he had found all these missionaries "properly employed in their respective stations," but that he had proposed some changes in the disposition of the old missions, which could probably be brought about the ensuing year, and that he also projected some new missions. Writing

---

[1] In the autumn of 1773, Mr. Eagleson, of the Cumberland mission, visited Prince Edward Island and began the first mission there, which in 1775 was taken up by the Reverend Theophilus Des Brisay, who remained for forty-six years rector of the parish. St. Paul's Church, Charlottetown, has on its walls memorial tablets to Lieut.-Col. Sir Aretas Young, Kt., Lieut.-Col. Peter Des Brisay Stewart, Sir Donald Campbell, Bart., Lieut.-Governor of Prince Edward Island, who died in 1850; John Stewart, Esq., Rev. Theophilus Des Brisay, General Edmund Fanning, LL.D., Lieut.-Governor, first of Nova Scotia, then, for nearly nineteen years, of Prince Edward Island; Captain Frederick Augustus Fanning, his son, H. M. 22d Foot; Hon. Thomas Heath Haviland, and other distinguished persons.

to his friend, Bishop White, of Pennsylvania, shortly after his consecration, he says: "I found the state of this province nearly such as I imagine you found that of your diocese—in great want of the superintending care and inspection of a bishop; and much need I have of the divine aid to enable me to discharge the duties of this station—much prudence, judgment, temper, and zeal guided by discretion are required. I have the same authority given me over the clergy that bishops have in England over their clergy; but the temporal powers vested in English bishops by the constitution are withheld; and this by my own choice, for I drew up the plan that was adopted." Of his methods with his clergy he later writes Bishop White: "A stranger who read this letter would be apt to think I am an asserter of high Episcopal prerogative. But my clergy will unanimously testify that nothing of this appears in my conduct. I treat them as brethren—give them any assistance and consolation in my power—live in love and harmony with them, and use no other expedient than persuasion and example in the exercise of my authority." Here, indeed, is the keynote of

Bishop Inglis' episcopate. The "superintending care," he speaks of in his letter to Bishop White, he faithfully gave all the missions he could reach, in his vast field. Before his death, and many times, he visited the greater part of these missions in the various provinces under his spiritual control, giving personal fatherly advice and sympathetic aid to the struggling churches and hard-working missionaries of the Church whose first colonial bishop he had become.

In 1790, to aid him in his work in the scattered province of New Brunswick, he appointed Dr. Samuel Cooke commissary for that part of the diocese, and during the last years of his life, as during his successor, Bishop Stanser's long absence in England, his son, Reverend John Inglis, acted as commissary for the diocese, performing all the acts that a presbyter could possibly perform. After his death, for seven years, owing to Bishop Stanser's ill health, and consequent absence in England, the diocese was practically without a bishop, and its interests suffered. Yet in 1824, when Bishop John Inglis was appointed to his father's see, the clergy of Nova Scotia numbered twenty-eight, of New Brunswick, eighteen, of Prince Edward Island, two, of Newfoundland, seven, and of Bermuda one.

To his episcopate Dr. John Inglis brought a thorough acquaintance with the diocese over which he was placed, and a deep interest in its welfare. The report of the S. P. G. for 1825 says that "the consecration of the Right Reverend John Inglis, D.D., and the appointment of his lordship to the diocese of Nova Scotia, has placed the ecclesiastical concerns of that diocese under a more favorable aspect than it had enjoyed for a considerable length of time." One of the first acts of this bishop was the erection of four archdeaconries within his diocese, the Reverend Robert Willis, missionary at Halifax, being made Archdeacon of Nova Scotia, the Reverend George Best, missionary at Fredericton, Archdeacon of New Brunswick, the Reverend George Coster, Archdeacon of Newfoundland, and the Reverend A. G. Spencer, Archdeacon of Bermuda. The practical wisdom of this will at once appear. By means of his archdeacons, the bishop was able to keep in touch with the remoter parts of his diocese and to exercise a supervision which, otherwise, would have been far from possible. In 1826 he visited the whole of his diocese, except, perhaps, Prince Edward Island. In Bermuda, where no bishop had ever been before, and where there were now nine parishes and parish churches, and four resident clergymen, he administered the rite of confirmation to twelve hundred persons. Then he went to Newfoundland, where he carefully inspected the missions, founded in that island at different times since 1703. Later, he turned his attention to the eastern part of Nova Scotia, Cape Breton, and the Gulf Shore, the total number confirmed at this visitation being four thousand three hundred and sixty. In 1828, he again visited Newfoundland, where he consecrated eighteen churches and twenty burying grounds, confirmed, it is said, two thousand three hundred and sixty-five persons, and travelled five thousand miles. The number of persons confirmed at this time is very large, but it will not seem so remarkable when it is remembered that for almost ten years there had been no confirmations held in the diocese.

Between 1825 and 1838, is the period of most marked growth in the whole history of the diocese.[1] King's College was then supplying clergy for the places of the aged rectors who were falling off and for new missionary fields, so that there was no anxious waiting for clergy to be sent from England; and with increasing prosperity in the province and a multiplying population, in every direction new congregations were being organized and new churches built.

During all these years the faithful S. P. G. bore the chief financial burden of the Church in Nova Scotia. At the time of Bishop John Inglis' consecration, the diocese was drawing from its treasury nearly twelve thousand pounds a year. After a time, however, a gradual diminution began in the parliamentary grant to the Society for the support of the clergy in North America, and in 1834, the allowance had dwindled to four thousand pounds sterling. That year, an arrangement was made between the Society and the Government, whereby the reduced salaries of those missionaries already in Nova Scotia, should be paid

---

[1] "A Sketch of the Rise and Progress of the Church of England in the British North American Provinces," by Thomas B. Akins, D.C.L., p. 56.

directly by parliamentary grant, while they lived, or remained in the colony; and the Society accordingly transferred them to the Crown. At the present time, there is but one church in the peninsula of Nova Scotia, the church at Shelburne, which receives an allowance from the British Government under this act of transfer, while there are nine which are still aided, in greater or smaller sums, by the Society itself.

Statutes passed in 1758, and later, had provided for the erection of parishes throughout Nova Scotia by order of the governor and council, and the appointment of church-wardens and special vestries in each parish, with corporate powers to hold lands for the benefit of the parish church. To the Church lands of Nova Scotia we have already referred. Shortly after the transfer of the Society's missionaries to the crown in 1834, and the reduction of their salaries, an attempt was made in England to induce the provincial governments to alienate the clergy reserves throughout the whole of British North America, without stipulating for the appropriation of any part of them to the purposes for which they were originally set apart in 1791, or stipulating even for a nominal equivalent. In Prince Edward Island in 1836, this was really effected, and the Church lands were sold for four thousand pounds currency and the proceeds applied to other than Church uses. An appeal was soon made to the Archbishop of Canterbury, with the result that the proceeds were restored to the Church and made a fund for the support of the Church of England schools, under the direction of the bishop and the governor. In 1839 the Nova Scotia government passed a law declaring that all school lands should be vested in trustees, for the general purposes of education, but the British Government refused to sanction it, and declared, after hearing the opinion of counsel in England, as to the rights acquired by the S. P. G., that all school-lands already occupied and improved should be preserved to the Church. Lord John Russell, in his dispatch, even expressed doubts whether it would not be proper to admit the claims of the Church to a portion of the lands yet unoccupied.

In 1817, the S. P. C. K. began to extend its usefulness in North American dioceses by forming district committees in aid of its funds, and for the distribution of books and tracts. In its liberality, of course, Nova Scotia shared, and her missionaries' hearts were many times gladdened by the receipt from England of valuable boxes of books for use in their work. In 1837, a Church Diocesan Society was established in the province, to raise funds for books and tracts for destitute missions, to assist students for the ministry, and to aid in the erection and enlargement of churches and chapels. The usefulness of this society was very great, but in 1876 its funds were vested in the Diocesan-Synod, in trust, to be held and managed for the several purposes for which they had previously been held by the society. The various sources from which parishes now receive aid are, the British Government, the Society for the Propagation of the Gospel, the Board of Home Missions, the Church Woman's Missionary Association, the Colonial and Continental Church Society, and the Church Endowment Fund.

In the latest report issued by the Boards of Home and Foreign Missions, the number of parishes in the diocese is given as ninety-four,

The Church's Growth.   225

and the number of clergy, including the professors of King's College, as a hundred and sixteen. The diocese of Fredericton now contains seventy-seven parishes and seventy clergymen. The officers of the diocese of Nova Scotia, besides the bishop, are a dean, three archdeacons, four canons and an honorary canon, and nine rural deans. There is as yet no cathedral, though the corner-stone of one was laid by the Metropolitan of Canada, August 12, 1887.

Other clergymen in the diocese before 1830, exclusive of the first missionaries and the Loyalist clergy were: The Reverends Thomas Adin, Jerome Alley, H. Nelson Arnold, Samuel Bacon, Edward Lewis Benwell, George Best, Charles Blackman, William Bullock, John Burnyeat, John Burt, F. H. Carrington, John Chapman, James Cochran, William Cochran, James Cookson, Frederick Coster, George Coster, George Cowell, Theophilus Des Brisay, Alfred Gilpin, Edward Gilpin, Archibald Gray, Benjamin Gerrish Gray, J. W. D. Gray, Thomas A. Grantham, H. Hayden, Charle Ingles, James Jackson, —— Jacob, Louis Charles Jenkins, T. J. Laugharne, Thomas Lloyd, John Millidge,

James Milne, Christopher Milner, Raper Milner, George E. W. Morris, Robert Norris, David Ormond, A. D. Parker, Cyrus Perkins, Charles Porter, Walter Price, James Shreve, Alexander C. Somerville, James Somerville, A. G. Spencer, Samuel Thomson, Skeffington Thomson, William Twining, R. Fitzgerald Uniacke, A. V. Wiggins, Gilbert L. Wiggins, Robert Willis, Edward Chapman Willoughby, Edward Wix, Abram Wood, Joseph Wright.

CHAPTER XIII.

LATER BISHOPS.

THE RIGHT REVEREND ROBERT STANSER, D.D., SECOND BISHOP OF NOVA SCOTIA.

ON the resignation by Dr. Breynton of the rectorship of St. Paul's, the Reverend Robert Stanser, an English clergyman, was recommended to the parish as his successor. Mr. Stanser, of whose antecedents little is known in Nova Scotia, left London, June 1, 1791, for his new charge, into which he was inducted early in the autumn. The report of the S. P. G. of the next year contains the following notice of his induction: "The Reverend Mr. Stanser, who succeeded the Reverend Dr. Breynton, the Society's old and most respectable missionary at Halifax, has acquainted the Society of his having been instituted into that parish by the bishop of Nova Scotia, and legally inducted by the church-wardens, and that he had received every mark of attention, which he could expect or desire." In 1799, on the occasion of Mr. Stanser's second visit to England, it was voted unanimously by the parish, "That the thanks of the parishioners be given to the Reverend Mr. Stanser for his diligent, faithful, and conscientious discharge of the parochial duties, as also for his assiduous and affectionate attention to his parishioners during his residence among them. And that the church-wardens and vestry furnish him with a certificate expressive of the affectionate esteem of the parish, and of their high sense of his pious, diligent, and faithful discharge of his various duties as pastor of this parish from his first induction thereinto, in the year 1791, to this present period." Indeed, Dr. Stanser seems to have been, during his whole term of office, a faithful and efficient pastor, and to have grown every year more and more liked by his parishioners. Dr. Hill speaks of him as "very much beloved and, in the ordinary acceptation of the word, highly popular." In 1815 Bishop Charles Inglis died, and as has already been stated, Dr. Stanser was recommended by the provincial legislature as the most suitable person to succeed to the episcopate. The Archbishop of Canterbury preferred the Reverend John Inglis, and it is said that he received Dr. Stanser "not only with coldness but with a brusque if not rude manner." Dr. Stanser was consecrated by the Archbishop of Canterbury in 1816, and soon after his consecration returned to Halifax, but owing partly to the death of his wife, which had occurred in the preceding year, partly to the severity of the climate of Halifax, his health was too poor to admit of his entering very fully upon his work, and he almost immediately went back to England, where he remained until his resignation was accepted in 1824. During this time Dr. John Inglis performed the duties of ecclesiastical commissary, but he could not confirm or ordain, and for the long term of seven years every candidate for the ministry in Nova Scotia had to go for ordination, either to England or to Lower Canada. Fortunately the Church of England does not make confirmation an indispensable pre-requisite of Holy Communion, so even without the administration of the rite of confirmation the Church grew. The disadvantage of having no resident bishop was, however, very great, and Dr. Stanser himself urged the Imperial Government, time and again, to accept his resignation. One of the reasons for the Crown's unwillingness to do this was probably its fear that such a precedent might open the way to the resignation of their sees and their seats in the House of Lords by bishops in England. This, at least, is Dr. Hill's opinion in the account of the matter given by him. A somewhat different statement, however, was made by Earl Bathurst in a speech in the House of Lords in 1828. This nobleman said that he had advised Bishop Stanser to resign, but that the latter had replied that "he had but very little private fortune, and could not give up the emoluments derivable from his ecclesiastical offices." Color is given to this version of the story by Earl Bathurst's recommending the governments of Nova Scotia and New Brunswick to pension him, which they did, the former province granting him three hundred and fifty pounds a year, the latter two hundred and fifty, the S. P. G. adding two hundred more.[1] When Bishop Stanser resigned, Dr. John Inglis was appointed, as he should

---

[1] See Mr. H. Y. Hind's "University of King's College," pp. 60, 61.

have been, seven years before, to the Nova
Scotia see. A point of some little interest was
settled during Dr. Stanser's episcopate. It
was at first a question whether colonial bishops should or should not be called "lord bishops," and be addressed as "my lord," and
"your lordship." The prince regent set the
matter finally at rest by saying to Bishop
Stanser when the latter was presented to His
Royal Highness at a levee: "I am glad to see
your lordship," or "How do you do, my lord
bishop?" Bishop Stanser died in London in
1829. His wife, of whom there are few notices,
is said to have been an amiable and lovely woman. When she died the congregation of St.
Paul's erected a very chaste monument to her
memory in the church of which Dr. Stanser had
for so long been the faithful and earnest rector.

The Right Reverend John Inglis, D.D., Third Bishop of Nova Scotia.

The Reverend John Inglis, who became the
third bishop of Nova Scotia, was one of the
three children, of whom Mrs. Inglis in 1776
writes, as her "three helpless babes." He was
born in New York in 1776, and at ten years of

age began his studies in the academy at Windsor, among the first seventeen who entered the school. His later education was obtained at King's College, Windsor, of which institution he was one of the many pre-charter students.

In 1796, Bishop Charles Inglis writes that, "as soon as this horrid war is over," he intends to send his son to Oxford to finish his education, but whether he carried out his plan or not is nowhere told. In 1810, John Inglis was ordained by his father the second minister of the parish in Aylesford, a church having been built there, in great measure through the influence of Mr. James Morden, in 1790. July 31, 1800, he was made a justice of the peace for Aylesford, and the same year he seems to have gone to England, for Sir John Wentworth, writing to the Under Secretary of State on some important matter, says: "This will be presented to you by Mr. Inglis, only son of our bishop. He is a sensible, discreet gentleman." In Aylesford he remained from 1801, until the resignation of Dr. Breynton of the rectorship of St. Paul's, when he removed to Halifax. During the last years of his father's life, as has been said, he acted as ecclesiastical commissary, and at his entrance on the rectorship of St. Paul's, the S. P. G., "as a mark of the very high opinion entertained by the Society of his important services in the active superintendence of the diocese during the long illness of the late bishop, agreed to advance his salary £200 per annum; and in consideration of the very laborious duties attached to the mission, deemed it expedient to allow £100 per annum for an assistant at St. Paul's." Among the honors conferred by the province on Mr. Inglis, was his appointment to the legislative council in 1825, and also to the chaplaincy of the house of assembly, February 18, 1817.

On the death of Bishop Charles Inglis many people supposed that his son, who for some years had so efficiently acted as commissary, would be his successor. Mr. Inglis naturally thought so himself, and soon prepared to go to England. But the same vessel that took him across the Atlantic took also a memorial, drawn up by the Honorable Hezekiah Cogswell and other influential persons, and signed by the council and the assembly, requesting the Home Government to appoint Dr. Stanser, the popular rector of St. Paul's, bishop instead. To the evident chagrin of the Archbishop of Canterbury the prayer of the Nova Scotia legislature was granted, and Dr. Stanser was elected to the vacant bishopric. "Mr. Inglis," says Dr. Hill, "bore the disappointment with dignity, came back to the discharge of his duties with a good spirit, and was elected the third rector of St. Paul's." This was in 1816. After seven years, on account of ill health, Bishop Stanser resigned and Dr. Inglis, who, during the bishop's protracted absence in England had continued to act as commissary, was at once appointed. In 1824, he sailed for England, was consecrated at Lambeth on Palm Sunday, March 27, 1825, and the 19th of November, with his wife and daughters, arrived in Halifax harbor, in His Majesty's ship " Tweed." Next day he landed in the admiral's barge, "under a salute of cannon and ringing of bells," and on the 11th of December was sworn in a member of the council, under a mandamus, and took the seat next after the president, being complimented in addresses from many of the inhabitants of Halifax, the graduates of King's college, of which he was a governor, and other persons.[1] For twenty-five years he administered the diocese, lovingly, wisely, and well; but at last in November, 1849, on one of his visitations, at Mahone Bay he was attacked with fever, of which he was ill for months. When he grew better he went to England, but his work was done, and he died in London, October 27, 1850. Although a memorial tablet, similar to that erected for his father, was placed to his memory in St. Paul's Church, Halifax, his body does not lie there, but in Battersea churchyard, London. Bishop John Inglis' income from his see is said to have been about eleven thousand five hundred or twelve thousand dollars per annum, but his travelling expenses were so great, his hospitality was so generous, his gifts to charitable objects were so large, that he died poor. Of this very liberal salary, two thousand pounds sterling was paid by the Imperial Government from a parliamentary grant, which was to be continued during Bishop John Inglis' lifetime, four hundred pounds was from the American Bishop's Fund, administered by the S. P. G. and from the rental of a farm near Windsor, purchased for the diocese by the S. P. G.

---
[1] Murdoch : vol. 3, p. 539.

Bishop John Inglis' wife was Miss Cochran, daughter of the Honorable Thomas Cochran, speaker of the house of assembly and member of the legislative council, who died, August 26, 1801, "at an advanced age, and after a long and painful illness." Of Mr. Cochran's family, Thomas became a judge in Upper Canada, and was accidentally drowned, William was in the army and became a general, James was Chief-Justice of Gibraltar and was knighted; one daughter was married to Commodore, afterward Sir Rupert Dennis George, and another was Mrs. Inglis. The children of Bishop Inglis were, Dr. Charles, Sir John Eardley Wilmot, Thomas, a captain in the Rifle Brigade, one daughter married to an officer, Lieutenant Kilvington, and two who were not married. Lieutenant-Colonel Sir John Eardley Wilmot, the second son, was born in Halifax in 1814, and died at Hamburg, Germany, September 27, 1862. He was in the campaign in the Punjaub in 1848 and '49, and, his regiment being at Lucknow in the summer of 1857, on the death of Sir Henry Lawrence he succeeded to the command.

The Reverend Richard Avery writes of this

bishop: "Bishop John Inglis was the Chesterfield of the Episcopal bench. It was said of him that next to George IV., he was the most polished gentleman of his time."

M. Mariotti, a cultivated Italian, who during Bishop John Inglis' episcopate was for a short time professor of modern languages at King's College, describing his reception in Halifax when he first arrived in the province, says:

"Immediately on landing at Halifax and taking up my quarters at the 'Mason's Arms,' I called upon the bishop, who . . . took me out in his carriage to introduce me to Lord Falkland, the governor of the province, and asked me to dine with him that same evening, with Mrs. Inglis and the four Misses Inglis, and with such friends as he could manage to summon at a moment's notice. The bishop was a dapper, little man, with a lively face, on which the sense of what was due to his prelatic dignity was perpetually struggling to check the impulses of his bustling activity. There was something in him of the look and manner of Dean Stanley. The bishop's wife and four daughters had stateliness enough for the whole Episcopal bench in the Lords."

The Right Reverend Hibbert Binney, D.D., Fourth Bishop of Nova Scotia.

The Reverend Hibbert Binney was born in Sydney, Cape Breton, August 12, 1819, and educated at King's College, London, and at Worcester College, Oxford, where he graduated with classical and mathematical honors in 1842. After graduation, for five years previous to his consecration, he was a fellow of his college and tutor in mathematics there. In 1844, he received from Oxford the degree of M.A., and in 1851, of D.D. By the Bishop of Oxford he was ordained deacon in 1842, and priest in 1843; and March 25, 1851, was consecrated at Lambeth, fourth bishop of Nova Scotia. Bishop Binney's father was the Reverend Hibbert Binney, a clergyman of New England Puritan descent, who was graduated at King's College, Windsor, in 1811, and received from that college in 1827, the degree of D.C.L. He was at one time rector of the joint parishes of Aylesford and Wilmot, at another of the parish of Sydney, and in later life of the parish of Newbury, Berks, England. His mother was Henrietta Lavinia, daughter of the Honorable Richard Stout, of

Cape Breton. The first member of the Binney family in Nova Scotia was Jonathan Binney, of Hull and Boston, Massachusetts, who was born in Hull, January 7, 1725, and coming to Nova Scotia as a trader, became a member of the first legislature of the province, and later of the legislative council, and died in 1807. Bishop Binney married, January 4, 1855, Mary, daughter of the Honorable Judge William Blowers Bliss of Halifax, of a Massachusetts loyalist family, who bore him five children, two sons of whom are clergymen in England. He died suddenly in New York, April 30, 1887. There is a memorial window to him in the Hensley Memorial Chapel at King's College, Windsor, a church built in great part by his cousin, Edward Binney. Bishop Binney was a good man, and one in whom many persons who knew him best found much to like. He was, however, a pronounced high churchman, and with an English education, came to his diocese, not from the broadening and mellowing experience of parish life and the ministry of souls, but from a tutorship of mathematics. Bishop John Inglis, although an aristocratic, courtly man, was a person of genial qualities, had lived most of his life in Nova Scotia, and well understood the peculiarities of the mixed population the province contained. Accordingly, unfavorable contrasts were soon made between Bishop Binney and him, and it can hardly be said that the first impression the former made on the people at large ever wore off. For thirty-six years, however, he honestly administered the diocese, and his thorough business methods did much to put its affairs on a firm and settled basis. To the welfare of King's College, especially, his energies were directed, and that institution now owes much to his prudence and good judgment. With his death, the last link binding the Church in Nova Scotia formally to the Church of England was snapped, for henceforth the bishops of Nova Scotia were not to seek consecration in England, but at the hands of prelates on these shores. Bishop Courtney, in his first address to the Diocesan Synod of Nova Scotia says of his predecessor: "Bishop Binney came at an interesting and eventful time . . . of little more than canonical age to be consecrated, in sympathy with the revived ideas of Churchmanship, deeply impressed with the importance of grafting them upon the Church life of the diocese, with the prospect of a long life in which he might 'see of the travail of his soul and be satisfied,' what wonder is it that he found his task a hard and difficult one? That he succeeded so far, that he made for himself a name and reputation, that to those who knew him best he was a loving and tender friend, ready at all times with sweet sympathy and generous help; that the longer any one was associated with him the more he was respected and his character revered, must be to those who most mourn his loss, a deep satisfaction and an enduring comfort. A strong character, striving to express and impress itself in all ways open to it, he gained credit for high-minded integrity, strict conscientiousness, the acting always upon Christian principles, the endeavor to obtain by lawful means what he regarded as laudable ends; and, therefore, he secured the admiration of those who were animated by his spirit and agreed with his views; while those who opposed him, gladly acknowledged the blamelessness of his Christian life and the purity of the motives by which he was actuated. Of his unceasing watchfulness for the welfare of the diocese, his anxious endeavor to discharge his duty in the sight of God and with the approval of his conscience, his abundant labor, his unsparing giving of himself, his thought and study and prayer to prove himself 'a workman that needeth not to be ashamed,' a faithful Shepherd and Bishop of the souls committed to him, a wise counsellor, a courageous leader,—you all know better than I, for you were the witnesses of his actions, the objects of his care, his 'fellow-laborers unto the Kingdom of God.' He is of the number of those of whom it is said, 'Blessed are the dead that die in the Lord: yea, saith the Spirit, for they rest from their labors, and their works do follow them.'"

THE RIGHT REVEREND FREDERIC COURTNEY, D.D., FIFTH BISHOP OF NOVA SCOTIA.

The Reverend Frederic Courtney, D.D., was born in Plymouth, England, January 5, 1837. He was educated in part at Christ's Hospital, first at the preparatory school at Hertford, then the blue-coat school in Newgate street, London. After that he graduated in the first class from King's College, London, in 1863, when Dr. Jelf, Dr. McCabe, Bishop Ellicott, Dean Plumtre, and Archdeacon Cheetham were professors there. The degree of doctor of divinity was conferred on him by Racine College, Wisconsin. He was ordained priest by the Archbishop of Canterbury, in 1865; was curate of Hadlow, near Tunbridge, Kent, from 1864 to 1865; incumbent of Charles Chapel, now St. Luke's, Plymouth, from 1865 to 1870; incumbent of St. Jude's, Glasgow, Scotland, from 1870 to 1876, and assistant minister of St. Thomas' Church, New York, from 1876 to 1880. From New York he went to St. James' Church, Chicago, where he began his rectorship the first Sunday after Easter, 1880, remaining in that pastorate until March, 1882, when he accepted a call from St. Paul's Church, Boston.

He was consecrated at St. Luke's Church, Halifax, by Bishop Medley, Metropolitan of Canada, assisted by the Coadjutor Bishop of Fredericton, the Bishop of Ontario, the Bishop of Quebec, and the Bishop of Maine, on St. Mark's Day, April 25, 1888. Among the clergy present at his consecration were the following from the diocese of Massachusetts:

The Reverends Phillips Brooks, D.D., G. S. Converse, William J. Harris, D.D., and Horatio Gray of Boston; George Zabriskie Gray, D.D., of Cambridge, L. K. Storrs of Brookline, G. W. Shinn, D.D., of Newton, Roland Cotton Smith of Beverly, Charles S. Hutchins of Medford, and John Bevington, of Wareham.

CHAPTER XIV.

DISTINGUISHED LAYMEN.

ON no part of the American continent, it is safe to say, has the Church, within corresponding limits, had so many remarkable people among her lay members as in the diocese of Nova Scotia. For many years after the Loyalist emigration, the judges of the courts, the members of the council, and of the assembly, and those who filled the chief provincial offices, were men whose ability would have given them a prominent place in any country where they might have lived. And there has always been a dignity and high-breeding about Nova Scotian society that the Church, herself, has, of course, done her part towards creating and sustaining. Besides the names which have been given in the chapters on the Loyalist clergy in Nova Scotia, and on King's College, the following are some of the most important names in the local history of the Church in this diocese:

WILLIAM JAMES ALMON was surgeon to the Ordnance and Artillery. He married, August 4, 1786, Rebecca Byles, daughter of Dr. Mather Byles, her sister Anna being married at St. John, March 22, 1799, to Lieutenant-Colonel Thomas DesBrisay, of the artillery. One of their sons was Dr. William Bruce Almon, who married, January 29, 1814, Laleah Peyton Johnston, youngest daughter of William Moreton Johnston and sister of Judge James William Johnston. The present Dr. William James Almon of Halifax, Dominion Senator, is a son of Dr. William Bruce Almon. The late Honorable Mather Byles Almon, whose family has been one of the most important in Halifax, was a son of Dr. William James Almon and his wife Rebecca Byles. Dr. Almon died at Bath, England, February 5, 1817, aged sixty-two.

JAMES AUCHMUTY, of New York, brother of Reverend Dr. Samuel Auchmuty, went to Nova Scotia, where he became a judge of the Supreme Court. He had a son in the British army who was killed in battle in the West Indies.

THOMAS BARCLAY, son of Rev. Henry Barclay, D.D., Rector of Trinity Church, New

York, born October 12, 1753, was graduated at Columbia College and afterwards became a student of law in the office of John Jay. At the beginning of the Revolution he entered the British army under Sir William Howe, as a captain in the Loyal American Regiment, and was promoted to the rank of major by Sir Henry Clinton, in 1777. His estate being confiscated he went with his family to Nova Scotia, where he became speaker of the house of assembly and adjutant-general of the militia. He died in New York, April, 1830. He was the father of Colonel De Lancey Barclay, an aid-de-camp to George the Fourth, who died in 1826, having repeatedly distinguished himself in the imperial service, especially at Waterloo. In later life he had a pension from the government of twelve hundred pounds a year.

JOHN BEDLE, of Staten Island, New York, was born in 1757. In 1784 he went to St. John and was employed for a year or two in surveying that city. About 1794 he removed to Woodstock, where he was a magistrate for forty years. After the division of York county, he was a judge of the court of common pleas, and registrar of wills and deeds for the county of Carleton. His wife was Margaret Dibble, who bore him ten children. He died in 1838, aged eighty-three.

PETER BERTON, of Long Island, New York, went to New Brunswick in 1783, and became a judge of the court of common pleas.

CHRISTOPHER BILLOPP, of Staten Island, New York, in the Revolution commanded a corps of loyal militia, raised in the vicinity of New York City, and was taken prisoner by the Whigs, and confined in the jail at Burlington, New Jersey, his large property being confiscated under the act of New York. In 1783, he was one of the fifty-five petitioners for lands in Nova Scotia. He went to New Brunswick in 1784, and became a member of the house of assembly and of the council, and in 1823, was a competitor with the Honorable Ward Chipman for the presidency of the government. He died at St. John in 1827, aged ninety. His wife, Jane, died in that city, in 1802, aged forty-eight. His two sons were merchants in New York; his daughter Mary was the wife of the Reverend Archdeacon Willis of Nova Scotia; and his daughter Jane, of the Honorable William Black, of St. John.

Distinguished Laymen. 249

JONATHAN BINNEY, ancestor of the fourth bishop of Nova Scotia, was one of the members of the first assembly in 1758, and long a member of the council. His wife died on Friday, December 22, 1797, in her seventy-fifth year. His son, or grandson, Stephen Hall Binney, married at Preston, September 22, 1794, Susanna, daughter of Francis Green.

DANIEL BLISS of Concord, Massachusetts, a son of the Rev. Samuel Bliss, was born in 1740 and graduated at Harvard in 1760. He was one of the barristers and attorneys who addressed Hutchinson in 1774, and was proscribed under the act of 1778. He joined the British army, and after the Revolution, settled in New Brunswick, where he became a member of the council, and chief-justice of the court of common pleas.

JOHN MURRAY BLISS, son of Daniel Bliss, did not settle in New Brunswick until 1786. He was a lawyer, represented the county of York in the assembly, and in 1816 was elevated to the bench and to a seat in the council. In 1824, on the death of the Honorable Ward Chipman, President and Commander-in-Chief of the colony, he administered the government until the arrival of Sir Howard Douglas, a period of nearly a year. At his death in 1834, he was senior justice of the Supreme Court.

JONATHAN BLISS, of Springfield, Massachusetts, was born in 1742, and graduated at Harvard in 1763. He was a member of the General Court of Massachusetts in 1768, and one of the seventeen "Rescinders." Proscribed under the act of 1778, he went to New Brunswick, where he finally attained the rank of Chief-Justice, and also President of the Council.

SAMPSON SALTER BLOWERS, of Boston, graduated at Harvard in 1763, in a class celebrated for the number of Loyalists and judges it produced. He entered on the study of law with Hutchinson, then judge of probate and lieutenant-governor, and in 1770, was associated with Messrs. Adams and Quincy "in behalf of the British soldiers who were tried for their agency in the Boston massacre, so termed, in that year." Between 1774 and 1778, he was proscribed, and imprisoned, and on his release, went to Halifax where he became attorney-general, speaker of the house, a member of the council, and in 1797, Chief Justice of Nova Scotia. He retired from public life in 1833, and died in 1842. His wife was Sarah, daughter of Benjamin Kent, of Massachusetts.

ISAAC BONNELL, of New Jersey, was sheriff of Middlesex County, under Governor William Franklin, his intimate friend and correspondent. His property was confiscated and he went to Digby, Nova Scotia, where he became a merchant and a judge of the court of common pleas. He died in 1806, aged sixty-nine.

AMOS BOTSFORD, of Newton, Connecticut, a lawyer, was graduated at Yale in 1763. At the Revolution he went to New Brunswick, where he represented the county of Westmoreland for the remainder of his life. He was speaker of the house as early as 1792. He died at St. John in 1812, aged sixty-nine. His wife was Sarah, daughter of Joshua Chandler. His son, Honorable William Botsford, was appointed Judge of Vice-Admiralty in 1803, was a member of the council, and also a judge of the Supreme Court. His daughter, Sarah, was the wife of Stephen Millidge, Sheriff of Westmoreland, and his daughter, Ann, wife of the Reverend John Millidge.

JAMES BRENTON, of Rhode Island, went to Halifax, and was a notary public there as early as September, 1775. He was afterward a member of the council, and a judge of the Supreme Court. In 1800 he was appointed Judge of Vice-Admiralty. He married first, Rebecca Scott, secondly, Miss Russell, of Halifax. Edward, his only son by his first marriage, was, in 1835, a judge in Newfoundland. His son John, by his second marriage, was secretary to Admiral Provost on the East India station, and a captain in the British navy. His daughter Harriet became the wife of her cousin, Admiral Sir Jahleel Brenton, Bart., Rear-Admiral of the Blue, K.C.B. and K.S.F., who, from 1787 to 1789, was an officer of the "Dido," Captain Sandys, employed in surveying the coast of Nova Scotia.

ELISHA BUDD, of New York, ensign in the King's American Regiment, was at the siege of Savannah, and in several engagements in the South. His property was confiscated and he went to Digby, Nova Scotia, where he became a merchant and a justice of the court of common pleas. He died at Liverpool, England, in 1813, aged fifty-one. His wife was a daughter of Isaac Bonnell.

GEORGE BRINLEY was commissary and store-

Distinguished Laymen. 253

keeper general in the garrison at Halifax in October, 1797. His wife was a sister of Lady Wentworth and of Benning Wentworth. William Birch Brinley, his son, married Joanna Allen, daughter of John Allen, Esq., of Preston, Nova Scotia, and their only daughter was the wife of William Lawson, of Halifax. One of George Brinley's daughters was Mrs. Moody, the mother of Mrs. Gore, the novelist, who, at the death of Sir Charles Mary Wentworth, inherited the "Prince's Lodge" estate at Halifax.

JOSHUA CHANDLER, of New Haven, barrister-at-law, was graduated at Yale in 1747. His property, which he valued at thirty thousand pounds, was confiscated, and in 1783 he went to Annapolis. In March, 1787, he crossed the Bay of Fundy to St. John to meet the commissioners on Loyalist claims, and in a violent snowstorm perished near the New Brunswick coast. His son William and his daughter Elizabeth also died at this time. His sons Samuel, Charles, William (graduated at Yale in 1773), and Thomas were all in New Brunswick.

WARD CHIPMAN, of Massachusetts, was born in 1754, and graduated at Harvard in 1770. In 1775, he was driven from his house to Boston, and was one of the eighteen country gentlemen who next year were addressers of Gage. At the evacuation of Boston, he left and went to Halifax. Later, he removed to New Brunswick, where he became a member of the assembly, Advocate-General, Solicitor-General, Justice of the Supreme Court, a member of the council, and President and Commander-in-Chief of the colony. He died at Fredericton in 1824, and was buried in St. John. His only son, Ward, graduated at Harvard in 1805, was finally Chief-Justice of New Brunswick, and died at St. John in 1851. In August, 1860, the Prince of Wales, visiting St. John, occupied the Chipman mansion.

ENOS COLLINS, a member of the legislative council, who married, June 28, 1825, at St. Paul's Church, Reverend Dr. Willis officiating, Margaret, eldest daughter of Judge, afterward Sir Brenton Halliburton, was long the richest man in Halifax. His family were prominent members of St. Paul's.

JOHN CREIGHTON, lieutenant-colonel in the militia, lived at Lunenburg. His daughter Sarah was married, August 13, 1799, to Lewis Martin Wilkins, sheriff of Halifax County. His daughter Lucy was married, August 2, 1792, by the Reverend Mr. Money, to Hibbert Newton Binney, collector of customs for Halifax County. Colonel Creighton died May 28, 1826.

ROBERT CUNARD, of Philadelphia, Pennsylvania, was attainted of treason, and had his estate confiscated. He died at Portland, New Brunswick, in 1818, aged sixty-nine. His son Abraham, who became a prominent merchant in Halifax, and died in that city, was the father of Sir Samuel Cunard, the founder of the Cunard Steamship Line.

RICHARD CUNNINGHAM, of Windsor, probably a son of John Cunningham, appointed Indian Superintendent by Governor Parr, married "at the seat of Sir John Wentworth" in Halifax, August 22, 1809, Sarah Apthorp Morton, eldest daugther of the Honorable Perez Morton, of Boston, and niece of Lady Wentworth. The Reverend Dr. Gray officiated at this wedding. Richard Cunningham had one daughter, married to the Reverend John Storrs, long Rector of Cornwallis, and another to the Reverend Mr. Clinch. He had sons—John and Morton.

JAMES DE LANCEY, of Westchester, New York, son of Peter de Lancey and his wife, Elizabeth Colden, was sheriff of Westchester. At the time of the Revolution he was lieutenant-colonel commandant of a battalion in the regiment of his uncle, the senior Oliver de Lancey. At the peace he went to Nova Scotia and settled at Annapolis, where he died, in 1800, a member of the council. Martha, his widow, also died there in 1827, aged seventy-three.

MICHAEL FRANCKLIN, or Francklyn, a New England man, appears in Nova Scotia as early as 1752. In 1761 he was made a justice of the peace, and May 3, 1762, was appointed to the council. In 1766, shortly after the death of Governor Wilmot and before the arrival of Lord William Campbell, he was made lieutenant-governor, taking command of the province until the governor came. In 1768 he was appointed lieutenant-governor of the Island of St. John (P. E. I.), but continued to hold the office of lieutenant-governor of Nova Scotia until 1776, when Commodore Mariot Arbuthnot was appointed. Mr. Francklin rendered the province distinguished service. He administered the government several times, was agent for Indian affairs, and had a voice in all legislative concerns. His wife, born in 1740, was Susanna, daughter of Joseph Boutineau, of Boston, and granddaughter of Mr. Peter Faneuil of that city. He married her in Boston, January 21, 1762. They had ten children born between July, 1763, and December, 1780, of whom James Boutineau Francklin, Clerk of the House of Assembly for nearly forty-two years, was the eldest.

FRANCIS GREEN was born in Boston in 1742, and graduated at Harvard in 1760. He early took an ensign's commission in the 40th Regiment and was present at the siege of Louisburg. In 1776, he went to Halifax where he was appointed a magistrate. In 1777, he went back to New York, and the next year was proscribed and banished. For a time he was in England, but in June, 1784, he returned to Nova Scotia, and was appointed sheriff of the county of Halifax and senior judge of the court of common pleas. He was the second son of the Honorable Benjamin Green; his wife was Susanna, daughter of Joseph Green. His daughter, Susanna, who died in 1802, was the wife of Stephen Hall Binney.

THOMAS CHANDLER HALIBURTON ("Sam Slick"), a grandson of William Haliburton and his wife, Susanna Otis, who were married in King's Chapel, Boston, and afterward lived in Newport, Rhode Island, was perhaps the most eminent literary man Canada has ever produced. He was born at Windsor, December 17, 1796, entered King's College in 1810, was graduated in 1815, received from his alma mater the degree of M.A., in 1851, and was made a D.C.L. by Oxford University in 1858. Mr. Haliburton was early admitted to the bar of his native province, engaging in politics as well, and was made a judge of the Supreme Court in 1841. He resigned his judgeship in 1856 and went to England, where he entered Parliament as member for Launceston representing that county from 1859 to 1865. His great political service in Nova Scotia was his championship of the act abolishing restriction on the Roman Catholic religion. His best-known books are his "History of Nova Scotia," "Bubbles of Canada," "The Letter Bag of the Great Western, or Life in a Steamer," "The Old Judge, or Life in a Colony," "The Clockmaker," "The Attaché," "Wise Saws," and "Nature and

Human Nature." These writings are the works of a master of satire, yet a man of large, genial spirit. Judge Haliburton married first, Louisa, daughter of Captain Neville, of the 19th Light Dragoons; secondly, Sarah Harriet, daughter of William M. Owen, of Woodhouse, Shropshire, England, and widow of E. H. Williams of Eaton-Mascott, Shrewsbury. He died at Gordon House, Isleworth-on-the-Thames, August 27, 1865.

SIR BRENTON HALLIBURTON, KT., was the son of Dr. John Halliburton who came from Scotland to Newport, Rhode Island, as surgeon in a British war ship, and married there, Miss Brenton, daughter of Jahleel Brenton, and aunt of Admiral Sir Jahleel Brenton. He was baptized in Trinity Church, Newport, December 27, 1774, and came with his parents to Nova Scotia during the progress of the Revolution. He was educated for the law in England, returned to Nova Scotia to practise, and from 1833 to 1860, was Chief-Justice of the province. His wife was Margaret, daughter of Bishop Charles Inglis.

JAMES WILLIAM JOHNSTON, born in Jamaica, West Indies, August 29, 1792, was a son of William Moreton Johnston, a Georgia Loyalist, who, after the Revolution settled in Jamaica, and grandson of Dr. Lewis Johnston, a Scotchman. His brother Lewis, a physician, like himself a graduate of Edinburgh University, married a Miss Pryor, and lived for many years in Nova Scotia. His brother John married Laura Stevenson, daughter of the Attorney-General of Jamaica, and practised medicine in Annapolis, Nova Scotia. His sister Eliza was the wife of Judge Thomas Ritchie of Annapolis, the mother of Judge John W. Ritchie, of Halifax, and of Sir William Johnston Ritchie, Chief Justice of the Dominion of Canada. His sister Laleah was the wife of Dr. William Bruce Almon. James William Johnston was admitted to the Nova Scotia bar in 1813, and began to practise in Kentville. From Kentville he removed to Halifax, where he rose rapidly in his profession, and entering political life, became solicitor-general, attorney-general, judge in equity and at last in 1873, governor. When he received the last appointment he was in the South of France. He never reached the province, but died in England on his way home. For years Judge Johnston was the great conservative leader in Nova Scotia, as the Honorable Joseph Howe was the liberal leader. As has elsewhere been stated, he was one of the most prominent of those who seceded from St. Paul's Church and joined the Baptists. Of this denomination some members of his family are still devoted adherents.

GEORGE DUNCAN LUDLOW, of New York, at the time of the Revolution was a judge of the Supreme Court, and one of the most influential men in the colony. In 1783, he went to New Brunswick, where he was a member of the first council, and later, became the first Chief-Justice of the province. He died at Fredericton, February 12, 1808. Frances, his widow, daughter of Thomas Duncan, died at St. John, in 1825, at the age of eighty-seven. His daughter Elizabeth was the wife of the Honorable John Robinson of St. John.

JAMES MORDEN was a member of the old "Council of Twelve." He owned a fine estate in Aylesford, and it was he who induced Bishop Charles Inglis to settle there. Through his means the Aylesford Church was built in 1790.

JAMES PUTNAM, of Worcester, Massachusetts, a graduate of Harvard of 1746, studied law with Judge Trowbridge, and settled in Worcester, where he became one of the ablest lawyers in America. At the time of the Revolution he entered the British service, and in 1776, embarked with the army for Halifax, two years later being proscribed and banished. In 1784 he was appointed a judge of the Supreme Court in New Brunswick, and a member of the council. He died at St. John in 1789. John Adams was a student of law in his office.

BEVERLY ROBINSON, JR., of New York, was a member of the council of New Brunswick, and an important person in the province. The Robinson family was of the highest social standing in New York, and its members, unlike the Morris family, seem all to have been Loyalists. Colonel Beverly Robinson, senior, a son of the Honorable John Robinson, of Virginia, came to New York and married Susanna Phillips, of Phillips Manor, on the Hudson. During the Revolution he took an active part on the side of the Crown, and at the peace, with part of his family, went to England. His name appears as a member of the first council of New Brunswick, but he never took his seat. His sons were, Beverly, junior, Lieutenant-

Colonel of the Loyal American regiment, his brother-in-law Thomas Barclay having the rank of major; John, who was also a member of the New Brunswick council and treasurer of the province; Sir Frederick, G.C.B., who was an officer in the British army, and served under the Duke of Wellington; Sir William Henry, K.C.H., in the Commissariat of the British army; and Morris, also in the army. The younger Beverly Robinson married Nancy, daughter of Reverend Dr. Henry Barclay, John married Elizabeth, daughter of Chief-Justice Ludlow, of New Brunswick, and Sir William Henry married Catherine, daughter of Cortlandt Skinner, Attorney-General of New Jersey. Three of the brothers, Beverly, John, and Morris, have descendants in New Brunswick.

TIMOTHY RUGGLES, son of the Reverend Timothy Ruggles of Rochester, Massachusetts, was born in 1711, and graduated at Harvard in 1732. Before the Revolution he distinguished himself both at the bar and in politics, in 1757 being appointed associate justice of the court of common pleas, and in 1765, a delegate to the Congress of nine colonies at New York. As the Revolution progressed he became one of the most violent supporters of the Crown, and was accordingly fiercely hated by the Whigs. At the evacuation of Boston he accompanied the troops to Halifax, and some time after, became a proprietor of the town of Digby. He died at Wilmot, in 1795, aged eighty-five. One of his descendants is the Reverend John Owen Ruggles, of Halifax, and another Mr. Timothy Dwight Ruggles, an eminent lawyer and queen's counsel, of Bridgetown.

JONATHAN SEWALL, Attorney-General of Massachusetts, was graduated at Harvard in 1748. He was long an intimate friend of John Adams, and his friendship with that distinguished man was not interrupted even by the Revolution. In 1775 he went to England, and in 1788, having been appointed Judge of the Admiralty for Nova Scotia and New Brunswick, came out to Halifax. He died at St. John in 1796, aged sixty-eight. His wife was Esther, fourth daughter of Edmund Quincy, and sister of the wife of John Hancock. His son, Jonathan Sewall, became Chief-Justice of Lower Canada, and died at Quebec in 1840. His son Stephen was solicitor-general of the same province, and died at Montreal in 1832.

GILBERT STUART of Newport, Rhode Island, was the father of Gilbert Stuart the painter. In the Revolution his property was confiscated and he went to Nova Scotia. His wife was Elizabeth, daughter of Captain John Anthony, and his only daughter, Anne, became the wife of Henry Newton, collector of customs. He died at Halifax in 1793, aged seventy-five.

NATHANIEL RAY THOMAS, of Massachusetts, was graduated at Harvard College in 1751, and in 1776, his property confiscated, went to Nova Scotia and settled at Windsor, where he was collector of customs. His wife was Sally Deering, of Boston, and his only daughter was the wife of Judge Lewis Morris Wilkins. It is probable that through the Deerings his family was connected with Lady Wentworth. In 1789, Mr. Thomas was fined in Windsor for failing to attend church for three months. He died, August 12, 1823, aged sixty-eight. August 17, 1797, Lieutenant Charles Thomas, H. M. 7th Regt., "a cousin of Sir John Wentworth," was accidentally shot and killed by a brother officer. Lieutenant Thomas was a great favorite with the Duke of Kent, who lamented his death and erected a monument over his grave. His funeral was from Government House.

PROVO WALLIS was an officer of the dockyard, and married, September 29, 1788, Elizabeth Lawlor, of Halifax. His son the venerable Rear-Admiral Sir Provo W. P. Wallis, G.C.B., born at Halifax, April 12, 1791, is still living. His eldest daughter, Elizabeth Martha, was married June 31, 1813, to Lord James Townshend, Captain of H. M. Ship, "Aeolus," R.N.

Sir Provo W. P. Wallis, who is known as the "Father of the Fleet," was senior surviving lieutenant of the "Shannon" in her engagement with the "Chesapeake," and conducted the latter vessel into Halifax Harbor, in 1813. On board was the body of Captain James Lawrence, who distinguished himself in the American navy, and made immortal the words: "Don't give up the ship." Captain Lawrence's body was first buried in Halifax, but was afterwards removed to Trinity churchyard, New York, where an imposing monument was erected to his memory. Of Admiral Wallis, on the recent celebration of his one hundredth birthday, a newspaper said: "The world's history, it is believed, does not afford a parallel to his case. A man comparatively hale and hearty in 1891, who was a member of the fleet when mighty Nelson was yet winning his fame, when Trafalgar was yet in the future, who first smelt powder in 1805 and gained his first decoration in 1810, is a wonder indeed."

SIR JOHN WENTWORTH, BART., was governor of Nova Scotia from 1792 until 1808, and an ardent Churchman. Sir Charles Mary Wentworth, his son, the second and last baronet, who, however, spent little time in Nova Scotia, was made provincial secretary in 1808. Lady Wentworth's brother, Benning Wentworth, was made provincial treasurer in 1793, provincial secretary in 1796, and master of the rolls and register in chancery in 1800. He died in 1808, in the fifty-third year of his age.

A few other leading Church names in Nova Scotia and New Brunswick are: Allison, Armstrong, Barlow, Barrington, Belcher, Betts, Boggs, Bonnett, Butler, Campbell, Carman, Chaloner, Coster, De Blois, Denison, De Peyster, Desbarres, De Wolf, Dodd, Fraser, George, Grassie, Gray, Griswold, Hamilton, Harris, Hartshorne, Hazen, Hill, Jones, Kaulbach,

Leslie, Maynard, Merritt, Millidge, Muir, Newton, Owen, Palmer, Piper, Pryor, Ratchford, Ritchie, Roberts, Robie, Robinson, Ross, Slater, Starr, Thorne, Townsend, Tremaine, Twining, Van Buskirk, Vroom, Wallace, White, Wiggins, Williams, and Winniett.

CHAPTER XV.

OTHER RELIGIOUS BODIES.

THE earliest missions in Acadia were conducted by Jesuits sent out through the influence of Madame la Marquise de Guercheville in 1611. These were entirely unsuccessful, and the later conversion of the Indians to Roman Catholicism seems to have been effected, chiefly through the Franciscans, or Recollets, who took their place in 1619, and re-established themselves again in 1633. In 1753, the French had six churches in the peninsula of Nova Scotia, one at Annapolis, with Monsieur des Enclaves as priest, one at Cobequid, two at Pisiquid, one at Minas, and one at River Canard. The most famous priest ever in Nova Scotia, was Monsieur Louis Joseph de la Loutre, a worldly, scheming man and an implacable foe to Britain, who was in the province from 1741 until the expulsion of the Acadians in 1755, and to whose influence was in great measure due the continued refusal of these people to take the oath of allegiance to the English king. Besides him, at the time of the founding of Halifax, was Monsieur Antoine Simon Maillard, who, under the auspices of the Society of Foreign Missions in Paris, was sent out to Canada about the year 1734, and later was removed to Nova Scotia and Cape Breton, where he became Vicar-General of Louisburg, at its fall retiring to the woods and ministering to the people of the few Acadian and Indian villages between that and Miramichi. For a long time this priest, like de la Loutre, was an avowed enemy of the English, but in 1759 he made his peace with them, and on the invitation of the governor took up his residence at Halifax, and used his influence to conciliate the Micmacs, for which the government gave him a salary of two hundred pounds a year. He seems, likewise, practically to have renounced his Church, for when he died in 1762, the Reverend Thomas Wood attended his bedside and at his own request read the prayers from the Church of England Prayer Book, afterwards conducting his funeral, which was attended by all the chief inhabitants of

Halifax, and by many French and Indians. By an act of the first legislature, Roman Catholics were ordered at once to leave the province, but notwithstanding this oppressive act, in great measure justified by the long-continued opposition of Acadian priests to British rule, the Roman Catholic Church did not lose its hold in Nova Scotia, and in 1784 a church was built in Halifax itself. In 1881, the adherents of this Church in Nova Scotia numbered one hundred and seventeen thousand four hundred and eighty-seven; in New Brunswick one hundred and nine thousand and ninety-one; and in Prince Edward Island, forty-seven thousand one hundred and fifteen.

The first Protestant Dissenters in Nova Scotia, were probably either New England Congregationalists, or Scotch or Irish Presbyterians. Of both classes there were some in Annapolis long before the coming of the Cornwallis fleet. When Halifax was settled, enough New England people joined the colony to make a Congregational Church at once necessary; and in a letter to the Boston Weekly *News Letter*, of the date of June 14, 1750, a correspondent writes: "We shall soon have a large Church erected, and for the encouragement of Protestant Dissenters, a handsome lot is laid out for a Meeting-House and another for a Minister, in a very pleasant Situation." In a letter to the same newspaper, June 14, 1750, probably the same correspondent says: "Yesterday the Governour laid the Corner Stone of the Church which is now building, and which I believe will be the handsomest in America. And as soon as we can get a Dissenting Minister settled here, we shall have a handsome Meeting-House with a good Dwelling-House for the Minister, built at the Public Expense. I have subscribed to the support of Mr. Cleveland for two months, as have the Governour and most gentlemen here: and I believe we have Dissenters enough here at Present for four ministers." This "Mr. Cleveland" was the Reverend Aaron Cleveland, great-great-grandfather of Grover Cleveland, ex-President of the United States. He was born in Cambridge, Massachusetts, October 29, 1715, and graduated at Harvard College in 1735. His wife was Miss Susannah Porter, daughter of the Reverend Aaron Porter, of Medford, Massachusetts. December 15, 1750, a gentleman living in Halifax writes: "The Reverend

Mr. Cleveland is arrived here, and is well received by the Governour and other Gentlemen of the Place; he preaches every Lord's Day in the Afternoon in *the Church*, to good acceptance, and will continue to do so till a Meeting-house can be built."

The Congregational meeting-house in Halifax, to which reference is made in these extracts, was first named "Mather's Church," after the great New England Puritan divine; in after years it passed to Presbyterians of the Established Church of Scotland, and became known as St. Matthew's, the name it still bears. Of this church, Mr. Cleveland remained pastor only until the summer of 1754; then he resigned his charge and went to England for Holy Orders. Having been ordained, he returned to America and visited Halifax, but soon went to the United States, and died in Philadelphia, at the house of his friend, Benjamin Franklin, in August, 1757. After he left Halifax, Mather's Church was without a settled pastor for several years, but the Reverend William Moore was at last installed, some time before 1769. In the latter year, a German Presbyterian church was built in Lunenburg; and in 1770-71, a Lutheran church in the same place.[1] To the pastorate of the German Presbyterian church—"Dutch Calvinistic Presbyterian," it is called—Mr. Bruin Romcas Comingo was ordained in Halifax, July 3, 1770. This gentleman, who was born in Leewarden, Holland, in 1723, came to Nova Scotia with the German settlers in 1752, and died at Lunenburg, January 6, 1820. His ordination was the first Presbyterian ordination in the province. In 1785, besides the minister of the Lunenburg church, there were three Presbyterian clergymen in the province, Reverend James Murdoch settled at Horton, but preaching in many other places, Reverend Daniel Cock at Truro, and Reverend David Smith at Londonderry. In that year, a fourth minister, Reverend Hugh Graham, was sent from Scotland to the Cornwallis church, which had been started as a Congregational church; and in 1786, the first presbytery in Nova Scotia was formed at Truro, with the name of the "Associate Presbytery of Truro," its standards being those of the Presbyterian churches of Scotland, and its ministers declaring themselves

---

[1] Des Brisay's "History of Lunenberg."

to be subordinate to the "Burgher Associate Synod in North Britain."

The New England people who came to the province in greater numbers than before, between 1760 and '62, and settled on the lands of the exiled Acadians, were, of course, as a rule, Congregationalists. In 1769, as we learn by a memorial from the Cornwallis Congregational church to the Congregational churches of Boston and the neighboring towns, there were, in all, in Nova Scotia, six churches of this order, located at Barrington, Liverpool, Chester, Halifax, Cornwallis, and Cumberland, each with a pastor. Of the ministers of these churches, all but one were from New England, the Reverend Israel Cheever, of Liverpool, the Reverend John Secombe, of Chester, and the Reverend Caleb Gannett, of Cumberland, being graduates of Harvard, and the Reverend Benaiah Phelps, of Cornwallis, a graduate of Yale.[1] The remaining two were the Reverend Mr. Wood, of Barrington, and the Reverend William Moore, of Halifax, the former also a New

---

[1] Rev. Israel Cheever was graduated at Harvard in 1749, Rev. John Secombe in 1728, and Rev. Caleb Gannett in 1763. Rev. Benaiah Phelps was graduated at Yale in 1761.

England man, the latter a native of Ireland. With two Presbyterian clergymen, already mentioned, Mr. Murdoch at Horton, and Mr. Lyon at Truro, and possibly another Congregationalist in New Brunswick, these were all the Dissenting ministers at this time in the province.

In her early history in Nova Scotia, the Church, then, came into contact chiefly, among the various Christian denominations, with the Congregational body. The New England Congregationalists, as a rule, were deeply attached to their polity, which they then believed to be exclusively the New Testament plan, and were out of sympathy with the Church's worship; and, notwithstanding the moderate and conciliatory tone of feeling on the part of the government towards Dissenters, it is very clear that Churchmen never lost an opportunity of impressing upon the latter that they were in dissent. In their old home these people had had virtually an established church, but it was the one to which they still belonged, and in this new colony, with its formal adherence to the Church of England, in religious matters they no doubt often felt strangely out of place. How many of them soon came into the Church it is hard to say, but in every place where Church missions were established, there were no doubt some who felt the superiority of the Church's order and the beauty of her worship, and before long gave up their allegiance to Congregationalism, and knelt at her altars.[1] The greater part of them, however, were more or less influenced by the remarkable "revival," under the preaching of Mr. Henry Alline, the great Nova Scotia "New Light" preacher, which began in 1776 and lasted until his death in 1784. Henry Alline, the Whitefield of Nova Scotia, was born in Newport, Rhode Island, June 14, 1748, his parents, William and Rebecca Alline, having gone to that place from Boston, and later emigrated to Falmouth, Nova Scotia. He was a man stirred with the deepest emotions, and a preacher of the most fervid eloquence, which,

---

[1] The Cornwallis memorialists, in 1769, state that their people number a hundred and thirty-three families, not ten of which belong to the Established Church. They say that several of the "more loose and unstable" of their people have gone over to the Church, and unless they can get help in supporting their ministers, in a few years they will all be "Churchmen or nothing, in point of religion."

as in the case of Whitefield, few that came much under his influence were able to resist. It is probable that in Nova Scotia, owing to the scarcity of preachers and the necessary absorption of the people in their various callings, religious earnestness had much declined, and that the time was especially ripe for Alline's fervid preaching. Certain it is, that he stirred non-conformist Nova Scotia to its core, his work, as was natural in the eyes of the soberer Congregationalists, Presbyterians, and Church people, seeming to be attended with wild fanaticism and extravagance.[1] Under his influence, in Nova Scotia, New Brunswick, and Prince Edward Island, several important New Light Churches were formed, their principles, according to a later Presbyterian minister, being "a mixture of Calvinism, Antinomianism, and enthusiasm." After Mr. Alline's death, the societies he had founded, as a rule, gradually became Baptist churches, and settled into sober, conservative ways, the half-dozen old Congregational churches, with depleted memberships,

---

[1] See the S. P. G. report for 1790, where the principles and practices of the New Lights are said to be "subversive of all sober and rational religion."

keeping, as some of them are still doing, a trembling hold on life, or else changing into Presbyterianism and drawing into themselves whatever Scotchmen happened to be in their vicinity. The Baptist denomination, thus started, contained many of the most intelligent and influential New England families in Nova Scotia, and its history has been far from obscure. The towns and villages where Baptist churches were formed were desirably located, and were among the most progressive in the province; and when in 1826, or shortly after, the trouble in St. Paul's Church, Halifax, drove many of the most aristocratic families in the capital into independency, the principles of this body, evangelical, simple, and from Calvinistic Puritan premises, logical, the influence it had already acquired, and the promise of greater success it seemed to contain, led the former Churchmen of St. Paul's into the shelter of its fold. Henceforth, the Baptist body became one of the most important denominations in the province of Nova Scotia, occupying relatively a higher position there, it is probable, than anywhere else in the world. In 1881, this denomination was the third in point of numbers in the province, the Roman Catholics having the first place, the Presbyterians the second, and the Church of England the fourth.

The only remaining denomination of much size in Nova Scotia, is the Wesleyan Methodist, which stands fifth in point of numbers and has among its adherents, especially in Halifax, many persons of wealth and influence. The pioneer missionary of the Wesleyan body was the Reverend William Black, who preached, like his contemporary, Henry Alline, in most of the hamlets in Nova Scotia and New Brunswick and made many converts, one of his chief strongholds being Sackville, New Brunswick, where there was then a settlement of Yorkshire Methodists.

Between the New Light Congregationalists and the Methodists in these years, there was as little love as there was between the more conservative Presbyterians and Congregationalists and the disciples of Alline, but as was natural, the Church seemed to have less prejudice against the Wesleyans than against any other body. In 1785, a zealous Methodist minister named Garretson came to Halifax from New York, and soon after his arrival called on good Dr. Breynton, whose reception of him perfectly accords with the noble character of the first rector of St. Paul's. "You are on a blessed errand," said he, "I will do what I can to assist you, I desire to see the gospel spread." Nor was Governor Parr less kindly in his treatment of the minister. He spoke in commendation of Wesley, assured Mr. Garretson of his interest in the work the latter had come to Nova Scotia to do, and said: "Whenever you call for my assistance, if I can help you I will." In Newport, the Reverend William Twining had most cordial relations with the Methodists living near him, often preaching and administering the Communion in their church. The early growth of the Wesleyan body, however, was so slow that in 1800, there were only five ministers of this denomination in the Maritime Provinces. Among the converts to Methodism in Nova Scotia, were many New England people, but as a rule, the Methodists were chiefly English people who had settled here.

The early population of Nova Scotia, being of so high an order, the subject of education has always, necessarily, been foremost among the concerns of the province, and next to the propagation of their various religious views, has interested the leading Christian bodies. From the beginning, higher education here has been almost exclusively under denominational control, the Church having her schools at Windsor, the Roman Catholics theirs at Antigonishe and Halifax, the Presbyterian body its academy at Pictou and its college and divinity school at Halifax, the Baptists their college and preparatory schools at Wolfville, and the Methodists theirs at Sackville, just across the border of New Brunswick. The only one of the half-dozen colleges of the Maritime Provinc s that can fairly be regarded as undenominational, is the University of New Brunswick, at Fredericton, which is mainly under government control. Of the colleges in the present province of Nova Scotia, besides King's, there are but two that deserve especial mention— "Dalhousie," at Halifax, which, from its origin and with the present aims of those who control its fortunes, should in time be so far removed from denominational influence as to become pre-eminently the college of Nova Scotia; and "Acadia," at Wolfville, the respectable college of the Baptist denomination of the Lower Provinces.

In the chapter on King's College we have seen the fatal mistakes that were made in the early management of that institution, mistakes that large-minded people in all the subsequent history of the province have deplored, as tending to alienate people of other denominations from the Church, and to fix more firmly those narrow sectarian prejudices that are the bane of American Protestantism. Except for those early mistakes, King's College might, and probably would have become a university for the province, with an efficient staff of professors and with advantages for study greater than any Nova Scotia college can now possibly give. From 1816 until 1819, the governor of Nova Scotia was Lieutenant-General George Ramsay, ninth Earl of Dalhousie. An intelligent, broad-minded man, and evidently anxious to do something for the province during his short term of office; and seeing, as many Churchmen and others saw, the evil of the legislation which shut King's College against Dissenters, in 1817, as *ex-officio* president of the board of governors of the college, he made a strong effort to have the obnoxious statutes repealed. To this end, with the Nova Scotia government at their back, he and Chief-Justice Blowers united in a letter to the Archbishop of Canterbury, as patron of the college, begging his sanction to the proposed change. The Archbishop's answer was a prompt refusal: " To this proposition "—the proposition to confer degrees without requiring subscription to the Thirty-nine Articles—said he, " I cannot consent. The college was founded for the purpose of educating the youth of Nova Scotia in the principles of the Established Church; and the degrees conferred by it must be conferred in support of such principles." Failing in his purpose, Lord Dalhousie, who still saw clearly that one college was all that Nova Scotia could properly support, but who saw likewise the absolute need of an institution to which all young men, irrespective of denomination, might be freely admitted, obtained the sanction of the Imperial Government to the establishment of another seminary in Halifax, to which his lordship is said to have desired to give rather the character of a superior high school than of a university.

Other Religious Bodies. 285

The corner-stone of the building for the new school of learning was laid on the parade ground in Halifax, May 22, 1820, but the college, although largely endowed by government, was not opened until 1838 or '39, before its opening, however, every effort being made to unite it with King's on the proposed broader basis.[1]

It would seem that, with the history of the mistakes of King's College, Nova Scotians should have had their eyes open to the necessity for a large, generous provision for the educational needs of the province. But the end of mistaken college management had not yet come. Horton Academy was founded by the Baptists at Wolfville, in the beautiful " Land of Evangeline," in 1829, and went prosperously on for nine years, during which period, Dalhousie not yet having been opened, the need of a college where young men not Churchmen could obtain degrees became more and more felt. When

---

[1] The first fruitless attempt to unite the two colleges was made in 1823 and '24. This was followed by another, equally unsuccessful, in 1836, and this by a final attempt in 1885. In any broad view of education, the struggle to maintain three colleges in a province large enough for only one, is a vast mistake.

at last, in 1838, it was proposed to commence classes at Dalhousie, the Baptists, long since reinforced by the influential seceders from St. Paul's, with strong hopes of success, petitioned that a Baptist professor might be appointed to this college, which had been so liberally endowed from the public funds. No request could possibly have been more reasonable, but it was stupidly ignored, and the Baptists, having not only intelligence and wealth, but keen sense of justice, and indomitable energy and perseverance, now thoroughly aroused, determined to found a college of their own. This they did in 1839, of the ten members of the first governing body, at least five being men who had formerly been influential Churchmen. The staff of instruction at first comprised but two persons, the Reverend John Pryor and the Reverend Edmund Albern Crawley, both reared in the Church and graduated at King's College, but lately ordained as Baptist ministers.

The name of this college, whose first building, a fine classical-looking structure with Ionic or Doric pillars, stood on a commanding hill overlooking the wide " Grand Pré " and the blue basin of Minas, in 1841, was appropriately changed from "Queen's" to "Acadia."[1]

It is probably true that in late years the leading Dissenting bodies in Nova Scotia have often had ministers of greater ability, and sometimes of more thorough education, than the Church of England. This may especially be said of the Presbyterian Church, many of whose ministers are Scotchmen, or of sturdy Scottish ancestry, and with the advantage of having studied at the Scottish universities. The chief defect of the Churchmanship of Nova Scotia, is a lack of intellectual breadth, the result of the isolation of the diocese from great centres of thought and action, and there have consequently been many places where the attitude of the Church towards other religious bodies has been narrow and intolerant. In the United States, any pre-eminence the Episcopal Church may have attained, has been the result of an intelligent recognition by her members, of the great issues of thought on which religious

---

[1] Many Nova Scotians have studied at Edinburgh University, and at McGill, Montreal, while a considerable number of the graduates of Acadia have also taken degrees at Harvard, where they have ranked high as students of the college, or of the professional schools.

men have become divided, the broader intellectual movements back of present denominational differences. In Nova Scotia, the clergymen of the Church have too often made prescriptive authority and tradition do duty for clear thought and fair-minded appreciation of the positions of other Christian men. For this the complete cure can be found only in a broader university training, in which men of widely different opinions, and yet bound to respect each other's intellectual powers, shall come together in the freest social intercourse. It is, in great part, to this unrestrained mingling of able young men of all denominations in the various colleges and other institutions of learning, that the Churchmanship of the United States owes its well-recognized comprehensiveness and breadth. In Nova Scotia the Church may hold her own, but she can never gain greatly until her clergy come to understand that she is not simply the ancient Church of England, or the Church of the Tory people of the American Revolution, but that she is also a Church with infinite powers of adaptation to the intellects and hearts of nineteenth century men and women.

CHAPTER XVI.

ROYAL GOVERNORS OF NOVA SCOTIA.

COLONEL SAMUEL VETCH was adjutant-general of the expedition against Port Royal in 1710, received the keys of the fort of Annapolis Royal, October 5, 1710, and October 22d, became governor of the fort and the country, his titles being "Adjutant-general of all her Majesty's of Great Britain's forces, General and Commander-in-chief of all her troops in these parts, and Governor of the Fort of Annapolis Royal and country of L'Accady and Nova Scotia." He held the office until the twentieth of October, 1712, when General Francis Nicholson, who had commanded the expedition against Port Royal, was appointed. Colonel Vetch was the son of "a godly minister and a glorifier of God in the Grass Market," Edinburgh. He was one of the seven councillors who constituted the local government of the colony of Caledonia, a Scotch settlement established in 1698 at Darien, a little south of the Isthmus of Panama, but soon abandoned "as an unjustifiable encroachment on Spanish territory." In 1699, Mr. Vetch, with several others of the Darien expedition, came to New York, where, on the twentieth of December, 1700, he married Margaret, daughter of Robert Livingston, of Albany.

GENERAL FRANCIS NICHOLSON was lieutenant-governor of New England in 1688, lieutenant-governor of New York in 1689, of Virginia in 1690, and of Maryland from 1692 to 1698. In the latter year he was appointed Governor-in-Chief of Virginia. In 1710 he was appointed to command the expedition which brought about the surrender of Port Royal, and after that he went to England to solicit the crown to adopt measures for the conquest of Canada, in the abortive expedition for which he actively engaged. His commissions as General and Commander-in-Chief of the forces of Nova Scotia and Newfoundland, and as Governor of Nova Scotia and of the town and garrison of Annapolis Royal, are dated at Windsor Castle, October 20, 1712. The latter position he held until January 20, 1715, when Colonel Vetch was again appointed governor of Nova Scotia.

During this time, however, General Nicholson made but one short visit to the province, Colonel Caulfield being his lieutenant. Queen Anne died August 1, 1714, and George I. became king. It is said that General Nicholson was governor of South Carolina from 1721 to 1725. No other person was ever governor of so many different provinces.

COLONEL SAMUEL VETCH was again governor from October 20, 1715, the date of his commission, to August 17, 1717.

COLONEL RICHARD PHILIPPS.—His commission as Governor of Nova Scotia and of Placentia, and Captain-General of the forces, bears date August 17, 1717. In Newfoundland he succeeded Moody, and in Nova Scotia Vetch. He received a second commission September 11, 1728, and continued to be governor until 1749, though the lieutenant-governor and presidents of council actually administered the government a great part of the time. He was born in 1661, and as a young man is said to have been employed in distributing the manifestoes of the Prince of Orange among the troops encamped at Hounslow, for which service he was made captain. He served at the battle of the Boyne in 1690, became colonel of the Twelfth Regiment of foot, March 16, 1712, and of the Fortieth Regiment, August 25, 1717. He belonged to a family in South Wales, of whom Sir John Philipps, Bart., was the founder. He died in 1751, aged ninety.

In April, 1720, Governor Philipps formed the first council of Nova Scotia. The following gentlemen were chosen councillors: John Doucett, lieutenant-governor of the fort; Lawrence Armstrong, Paul Mascarene, Cyprian Southack, Rev. John Harrison, chaplain; Arthur Savage, John Adams, Hibbert Newton, William Skene or Skeen, William Sheriff, and Peter Boudrie. In August Gillam Philipps was added. Few English families having removed to the province, this council was composed of the officers of the garrison and public departments, and Mr. Adams was the only inhabitant admitted to the board. "Haliburton's History of Nova Scotia," Vol. I., p. 94.

Governor Philipps left Annapolis, August 27, 1731, and Lieutenant-Governor Lawrence Armstrong administered the government. The latter committed suicide the night before the sixth of December, 1739, and Mr. John Adams, as senior councillor, began to act as lieutenant governor. Major Paul Mascarene was in reality senior councillor, but he was in Boston at the time of Lieutenant-Governor Armstrong's death. He hastened back, however, and claimed the position. His right being conceded by the council, he assumed the administration of the government, and continued to exercise this function until 1749, when the settlement of the province was begun anew. In that year the Honorable Edward (afterward Lord) Cornwallis was sent from England with a colony of English settlers, numbering in all, it is said, 2,576 persons. Early in July many of these settlers were landed on George's Island, in Halifax harbor, but more on the peninsula where the city of Halifax now stands. Before the twenty-third of July (old style) twelve acres of the site of the intended town had been cleared, and Governor Cornwallis "expected to begin to erect his own house in two days thence, having a small frame and planks ready." On the twelfth of July (old style) Colonel Mascarene arrived at Chebucto, accompanied, as Governor Cornwallis had requested, by five of the council (a quorum). The next day the governor exhibited his commission to them and took the oath of office. He appointed a new council, who, that day, met with him on board the "Beaufort," transport, in the harbor and took the oaths. They were, as has previously been said, Paul Mascarene, John Goreham, Benjamin Green, John Salisbury and Hugh Davidson (Edward Howe being absent).

COLONEL, THE HONORABLE EDWARD CORNWALLIS (afterward Lord Cornwallis), son of Charles, third Baron Cornwallis, was born in 1712. He was colonel of the Twenty-fourth Regiment of foot, was appointed governor of Nova Scotia with a salary of one thousand pounds a year (the customary salary for the governors of Nova Scotia at this period), was M.P. for Eye in 1749, and for Westminster in 1753; was made a governor of the bedchamber, and finally became governor of Gibraltar. His twin brother, Frederick, was Archbishop of Canterbury. He was gazetted Governor of Nova Scotia, May 9, 1749, and sailed from England May 14th (old style). He was sworn in governor July 14, 1749.

COLONEL PEREGRINE THOMAS HOPSON, who had arrived from England July 26th, was sworn in governor on Monday, August 3, 1752. He was also commissioned Vice-Admiral. He sailed for England in the "Torrington," November 1, 1753, and the command of the province devolved upon the lieutenant-governor, the Hon. Major Charles Lawrence. Colonel Hopson was commander-in-chief at Louisburg when that place was restored to the French under the treaty of Aix-la-Chapelle. He came up with the army to Chebucto in July, 1749, and was soon sworn in senior councillor. After leaving Nova Scotia he was in active military service until his death, which occurred January 27, 1759.

COLONEL CHARLES LAWRENCE, appointed lieutenant-governor July 17, 1750, was made governor of the province July 23, 1756. Governor Hopson sailed for England November 1, 1753, and Colonel Lawrence probably administered the government until he himself was appointed governor. He was major in Warburton's regiment of foot, under Governor Hopson, in the garrison of Louisburg. He died Saturday, October 11, 1760. He never married. His administration in Nova Scotia covers the important period of the expulsion of the Acadians in 1755, and the resettlement of their lands in 1760–62 by New England people.

HENRY ELLIS, ESQ., who had been governor of Georgia in 1756, was appointed governor of Nova Scotia in the spring of 1761. He was in England at the time, and arrangements were made by the council in Nova Scotia for his reception, but for some reason he never came out. Chief-Justice Jonathan Belcher took the oath as lieutenant-governor, November 9, 1761, and the Hon. Colonel Montague Wilmot, September 26, 1762.

THE HONORABLE COLONEL MONTAGUE WILMOT, who took the oath of office as lieutenant-governor September 26, 1762, was appointed governor, October 8, 1763. By a proclamation dated at St. James, October 7, 1763, the islands of St. John and Cape Breton, or *Isle Royale*, "with the lesser islands adjacent thereto," were annexed to the government of Nova Scotia. Governor Wilmot died, May 23, 1766.

THE RIGHT HONORABLE LORD WILLIAM CAMPBELL, youngest son of the fourth Duke of Argyle, was sworn in governor, November 27, 1766. He had been appointed Captain-

General and Governor-in-Chief of South Carolina in the room of Lord Charles Greville Montague, in June, 1773. He married, in 1763, Sarah, daughter of Ralph Izard, of Charleston, S. C. In 1764 he was a member of the English House of Commons.

MAJOR FRANCIS LEGGE, a relation of the Earl of Dartmouth, was appointed Captain-General and Governor-in-Chief of Nova Scotia in June, 1773. He was sworn in, October 8, 1773. His administration was not successful. He left the province in 1776, but continued to hold the office for some years longer, during which its duties were administered successively by Lieutenant-Governors Mariot Arbuthnot, Richard Hughes, and Sir Andrew Snape Hamond.

JOHN PARR, ESQ., took the oaths of office October 19, 1782. He was commissioned Captain-General and Commander-in-Chief and also Vice-Admiral. Sir Andrew Snape Hamond, the lieutenant-governor, had expected the office, and feeling himself aggrieved, resigned his lieutenant-governorship, October 8, 1782. It was during Governor Parr's administration that the chief Loyalist emigration took place. He ceased to be governor in October, 1786, on the appointment of Lord Dorchester as Governor-General of all the British provinces in America. On the fifth of April, 1787, the king's commission was read in council appointing him lieutenant-governor. After the appointment of a Governor-General over all the provinces, the governors of the several provinces bore the title of lieutenant-governor, while they administered provincial affairs nearly as independently as before. The Governor-General on his appointment was obliged to take the oath of office for each separate province. Lieutenant-Governor Parr died after a short illness on Friday, November 25, 1791, in his sixty-sixth year.

JOHN WENTWORTH, ESQ., of New Hampshire, afterward Sir John Wentworth, Bart., a surveyor of his majesty's woods and forests in North America, who had been lieutenant-governor of New Hampshire, arrived at Halifax on Saturday, May 12, 1792, in H. M. frigate "Hussar," Rupert George, Esq., commander, after a five weeks' voyage from Falmouth, England. On Monday, May 14th, at one o'clock, he was sworn into office. In 1795 he was created a baronet, and June 16, 1796, he was still further honored with the privilege of wearing in the chevron of his arms two keys as an emblem of his fidelity. In 1808 he resigned his office, and the thirteenth of April of that year Sir George Prevost was sworn in, his successor. From June 1, 1808, until his death, he received a pension of five hundred pounds per annum. He was a son of Governor Mark Hunking and Elizabeth Rindge Wentworth, was baptized August 14, 1736-37, graduated at Harvard College in 1755, and received the degree of M.A. there in 1758. He married at Portsmouth, November 11, 1769, his cousin, Mrs. Frances (Wentworth) Atkinson, widow of Theodore Atkinson, jr. Their only son who lived was Sir Charles-Mary Wentworth, at whose death the baronetcy became extinct. Sir John died at Halifax, April 8, 1820; Lady Wentworth died at Sunning Hall, Berkshire, England, February 14, 1813, in her sixty-eighth year. Benning Wentworth, brother of Lady Wentworth, and Sir Charles-Mary were successively secretaries of the province.

The period of Governor Wentworth's incumbency of this office, owing to the residence in the province at this time of the Duke of Kent, Queen Victoria's father, is the most conspicuous of any in the history of Nova Scotia. The Nova Scotians were dazzled with the presence of royalty among them, and the Prince was personally very popular. At Government House, where great state was maintained, he was a frequent visitor, and it was during his residence that Governor Wentworth was created a baronet.

On Sunday, May 31, 1795, His Royal Highness and all the officers of the garrison went to the levee at Government House to congratulate Sir John and Lady Wentworth on the Governor's newly-acquired title. Prince Edward was in command of the forces in British North America in 1793, and was then resident at Quebec. He arrived at Halifax, from St. Kitts, May 10, 1794. He left Halifax finally August 3, 1800. During his residence here his brother, Prince William Henry, then a young naval officer, afterward King William IV., repeatedly visited the province. The presence for so long a time in Nova Scotia of the father of her majesty, Queen Victoria, has undoubtedly always given Nova Scotians a feeling of greater personal loyalty towards the Queen than they could otherwise have had. In later years at least three of her children and two of her grandchildren have visited the province. The "Prince's Lodge," about six miles from Halifax, was, as we have said, the property of Sir John Wentworth, who, in 1793, built a cottage on this beautiful spot, which he called "Friar Laurence's Cell." The Duke afterward enlarged and improved this cottage, which Sir John later occupied as his villa. The Prince of Wales visited the spot in 1860. The Duke of Kent was all his life particularly kind to Nova Scotians.

LIEUTENANT-GENERAL SIR GEORGE PREVOST, BART., was commissioned Lieutenant-General of Nova Scotia, January 15, 1808. He arrived at Halifax, April 7th of that year, and was sworn into office April 13th. In 1811, he was appointed Governor-in-Chief of Canada. On the twenty-fifth of August, 1811, he sailed for Quebec, and Alexander Croke, LL.D., Judge of Vice-Admiralty and a member of the council, was appointed to administer the government. Sir George was very popular in Nova Scotia.

GENERAL SIR JOHN COAPE SHERBROOK, K.B., was sworn in Lieutenant-Governor of Nova Scotia, October 16, 1811. He was appointed by the Prince Regent (King George IV.), June 18, 1816, Governor-in-Chief of all the British North American provinces, and on the twenty-eighth of June, Major-General George Stracey Smyth was sworn in as administrator of the government of Nova Scotia.

LIEUTENANT-GENERAL GEORGE RAMSAY, ninth Earl of Dalhousie, arrived in Halifax, October 24, 1816, and was at once sworn in lieutenant-governor. He, too, in 1819, was made Governor-in-Chief of the British provinces, succeeding the Duke of Richmond. As Governor-in-Chief, he took the oath for this province November 24, 1819. He was born in 1770, and succeeded his father in 1787, his son becoming Marquis Dalhousie. After he left America he became Governor-General of India.

LIEUTENANT-GENERAL SIR JAMES KEMPT, G.C.B., was appointed by the regent October 20, 1819. He arrived in Halifax with his suite June 1, 1820, and next day was sworn in lieutenant-governor. He was born in Edinburgh, in 1765, was captain of the 113th Foot, served in Ireland and Holland, and was made lieutenant-colonel in 1799. He was at one time in service in the Spanish Peninsula. In 1813 he was colonel-commandant of the 60th Foot, and was severely wounded at Waterloo. He was made Knight Grand Cross of the Bath and received several foreign orders. He was successively lieutenant-general (May 27, 1825), master-general of the Ordnance, and General (1841). He died in London, December 20, 1855.

SIR PEREGRINE MAITLAND, appointed lieutenant-governor of Upper Canada in 1818, his father-in-law, the Duke of Richmond, being Governor-General of Canada, was lieutenant-governor of Nova Scotia from 1827 till 1833. He was born in Hampshire, England, in 1777, and died in London, May 30, 1854. He entered the army in 1792, served in Flanders and Spain, and was at Waterloo in command of the First British Brigade. For his services there he was made K.C.B., June 22, 1815. From December, 1843, until September, 1846, he was Governor and Commander-in-Chief at the Cape of Good Hope. In 1846 he was made a general, and in 1852 a Knight Grand Cross of the Bath.

GENERAL SIR COLIN CAMPBELL, fifth son of John Campbell, of Melfort, and his wife Colina, daughter of John Campbell, of Auchalader, born in 1776, was lieutenant-governor, of Nova Scotia from 1833 till 1839. His army life began in 1795, when he became a lieutenant in the third battalion of the Breadalbane Fencibles, then commanded by his uncle. In 1801, he was gazetted a lieutenant in the 35th Regiment, and at once exchanged into the 78th, then in India. In Wellesley's advance guard against the Maharajah of Scindia, and the Rajah of Nagpore, he so distinguished himself that he was appointed brigade-major. After leaving India he received a company in the 75th Highlanders, and became aid-de-camp to the Duke of Wellington. From that time he steadily rose, until in 1814 he was made captain and lieutenant-colonel in the Coldstream Guards, appointed assistant quarter-master-general at the Horse Guards, and received a K.C.B. The next year he was attached to the staff of the Duke of Wellington as commander at head-quarters and was present at the battle of Waterloo. In 1818, he became lieutenant-colonel of the 65th Regiment, and in 1825, major-general. After he left Nova Scotia, he was Governor of Ceylon, from September, 1839, till June, 1847. He died in England, June 13th of that year, and was buried in the Church of St. James, Piccadilly.

VISCOUNT FALKLAND, P.C., G.C.H. (Sir Lucius-Bentinck Cary), born November 5, 1803, was returned heir to his father, ninth Viscount Falkland, in the peerage of Scotland, March 2, 1809. He was lieutenant-governor of Nova Scotia from 1840 to 1846. His first wife was Amelia Fitz Clarence, sister of the Earl of Munster, one of the natural children of King William IV., his second, Elizabeth Catherine, dowager duchess of St. Albans. He was created an English peer, May 15, 1832. He was governor of Bombay from 1848 to 1853.

SIR JOHN HARVEY, born in 1778, died in Halifax and was buried there March 22, 1852. He entered the army in the Eightieth Regiment, served in Holland, France, the Cape of Good Hope, Ceylon, and Egypt. In 1812 he was appointed deputy adjutant-general to the army in Canada, with the rank of lieutenant-colonel. After much other varied service Sir John became Governor of New Brunswick, and held the office from 1837 till 1841. From 1841 to 1846 he was Governor and Commander-in-Chief of Newfoundland, and in 1846 was appointed lieutenant-governor of Nova Scotia. He held this office until his death in 1852. He attained the rank of K.C.B., in 1838.

SIR JOHN GASPARD LE MARCHANT, son of J. G. Le Marchant, Esq. (a major-general in the army and the first lieutenant-governor of the Royal Military College), was a lieutenant-colonel, Knight of the first and third classes of St. Ferdinand, and Knight Commander of St. Carlos of Spain. He was born in 1803 and married in 1839. He succeeded Sir John Harvey as lieutenant-governor of Newfoundland in 1847 and of Nova Scotia in 1852.

AUGUSTUS CONSTANTINE PHIPPS, second Marquis Normanby and Earl Mulgrave, born on the twenty-third of July, 1819, entered the Scots Fusilier Guards in 1838, was comptroller and subsequently treasurer of the queen's household, and from 1858 to 1864 lieutenant-governor of Nova Scotia. He retained this office until his succession to his father's title, July 28, 1863, when he resigned. He was appointed governor of Queensland in 1871, of New Zealand in 1874, and of Victoria in 1878.

SIR RICHARD GRAVES MACDONNELL, K.C. M.G., LL.D., was lieutenant-governor from April, 1864, until some time in 1866. He was the eldest son of the Rev. Richard Macdonnell, D.D., provost of Trinity College, Dublin, and was born in 1815. He was graduated at Trinity College, Dublin, and was called to the bar of Ireland in 1838, and of England in 1840. He was Chief Justice of the Gambia in 1843, governor of the British settlements on the Gambia in 1847, and was for a long time occupied in exploring the interior of Africa. In 1852 he was governor of St. Vincent and Captain-General, and in 1855, governor-in-Chief of South Australia, where he made valuable explorations. From October 14, 1865, until 1872, he was governor of Hong Kong. He was made K.C.M.G., in 1871.

SIR WILLIAM FENWICK WILLIAMS, BART., K.C.B., perhaps the most illustrious of Nova Scotia's sons, was born at Annapolis, Nova Scotia, December, 1800. An an early age, through the interest of the Duke of Kent, he was placed in the Royal Academy at Woolwich. Entering the army he attained the rank of captain in 1840. His most distinguished service was in the Crimea, where he earned for himself an undying name as "the Hero of Kars." One of the gallant defenders of that town, during its four months' siege by Mouravieff, General Williams, on the twenty-ninth of September, 1855, gave the besiegers battle, and after a fierce conflict of eight hours' duration, defeated a force much larger than his own on the heights above Kars. The town fell, however, and General Williams was taken a prisoner, first to Moscow, then to St. Petersburg. He was almost immediately after created a baronet. In 1858 he was Commander-in-Chief of the forces in British North America. He administered the government of Canada from October 12, 1860, until January 22, 1861. In 1866 and '67 he was lieutenant-governor of Nova Scotia, his native province. He was made D.C.L. by Oxford, in 1856.

SIR CHARLES HASTINGS DOYLE, K.C.M.G., was lieutenant-governor from 1867 to 1873. He was the eldest son of Sir Charles William Doyle, C.B., G.C.H., and Sophia, his wife, daughter of Sir John Coghill, and was born in

1805. He was educated at Sandhurst, and entered the army as an ensign in the Eighty-seventh, his great uncle, Sir John Doyle's regiment. He was in service in the East, the West Indies, Canada, and Ireland. During the American war he commanded the troops in Nova Scotia, and showed great tact in the Chesapeake affair. He was appointed colonel of the Seventieth Regiment in May, 1868, and was made K.C.M.G., in 1869. After other service he died in London, March 19, 1883.

THE HONORABLE JOSEPH HOWE, born in Halifax, Nova Scotia, December 13, 1804, died there June 1, 1873. He was a son of John Howe, journalist, in 1775-76, editor with Mrs. Margaret Draper, of the *Boston News Letter*. His father, who was born in Boston in 1753, went as a Loyalist to Halifax, where he became King's printer, and died in 1835. Joseph Howe, himself, was an editor, a member of the council from 1848 to 1854, and provincial secretary. He superintended the construction of the first railways in Nova Scotia, and in 1863 was premier of the province. He was in the Dominion cabinet in 1869 as president of the council, and in 1870 secretary of state and superintendent-general of Indian affairs. May 10, 1873, he took the oath as lieutenant-governor of Nova Scotia, having been appointed May 1st. He died in less than a month; when his long-time political opponent, Judge James William Johnston, was appointed to the office. Mr. Howe was buried in Camp Hill Cemetery in Halifax.

THE HONORABLE JAMES WILLIAM JOHNSTON, Judge in Equity, M.L.C., attorney-general, solicitor-general, and representative in the legislature of Nova Scotia, was born in Jamaica, August 29, 1792. He was a son of Captain William Moreton Johnston and Elizabeth (Lightenstone), his wife, and grandson of Dr. Lewis Johnston, who emigrated from Scotland to Georgia, where he became a member of council. Judge Johnston was educated in Scotland, and admitted to the bar in 1813. He was in the south of France when, on the death of Lieutenant-Governor Howe, he received news of his appointment to the office. He accepted the appointment, but died on the way home.

SIR ADAMS GEORGE ARCHIBALD, K.C.M.G., son of Samuel, grandson of Judge James

Archibald, of the court of common pleas, was born in Truro, Nova Scotia, May 3, 1814. He was called to the bar of Prince Edward Island in 1838, and of Nova Scotia in 1839. He was a member of the executive council, first as solicitor-general from August 14, 1856, to February 14, 1857, then as attorney-general from February 10, 1860, to June 11, 1863. He was a delegate to England to arrange the terms of settlement with the British Government and the general mining association in respect to Nova Scotian mines, and also to obtain the views of Government relative to the projected union of the British-American provinces. He was sworn to the privy council July 1, 1867, but resigned in 1868. From May 20, 1870, to May, 1873, he was lieutenant-governor of Manitoba, and the north-western territories. From June 24 to July 4, 1873, he was Judge in Equity of Nova Scotia, and at the latter date was appointed lieutenant-governor of Nova Scotia. In 1873 he was one of the directors of the Canadian Pacific railroad under Sir Hugh Allan. He was knighted in 1885. Sir Adams Archibald is now living quietly at his home in Truro.

MATTHEW HENRY RICHEY, born at Windsor, Nova Scotia, June 10, 1828, is the son of the late Rev. Matthew Richey, D.D., a Wesleyan clergyman, born in Ireland. He was educated at the collegiate school at Windsor, Upper Canada College, Toronto, and at Queen's College, Kingston. He was admitted to the bar of Nova Scotia in 1850, was made a Queen's Counsel in 1873, and received the degree of D.C.L. from Mount Allison Wesleyan College in 1884. He was a member of the Dominion parliament for Halifax from 1878 to July 4, 1883, when he was appointed lieutenant-governor of Nova Scotia. He was mayor of Halifax from 1864 to 1867, and again from 1875 to 1878.

ARCHIBALD WOODBURY MCLELAN, born at Londonderry, Nova Scotia, December 24, 1824, was a member of the house of assembly from 1858 until the confederation of the British provinces in 1867. From that date until he was called to the senate, June 21, 1869, he was a member of the Dominion parliament. May 20, 1881, he was elected to the Privy Council of Canada. July 10, 1822, he was appointed minister of marine and fisheries and, December 10, 1885, minister of finance. January 27, 1887, he was made postmaster-general, and in 1888 became lieutenant-governor of Nova Scotia. He died June 26, 1890.

MALACHY BOWES DALY is the son of Sir Dominick Daly, of an old Irish family of County Galway. Sir Dominick was for twenty-five years Colonial Secretary, and representative for Megantic in the Canadian legislature. He was lieutenant-governor of Tobago, and later of Prince Edward Island, and then Governor-in-Chief of South Australia. His wife was Maria, daughter of Colonel Gore, of Barrowmount, County Kilkenny. Malachy was born at Marchmount, near Quebec, February 6, 1836, was educated at St. Mary's College, Oscott, near Birmingham, England, and married at Halifax, July 4, 1859, Joanna, second daughter of Sir Edward Kenny, of Halifax, formerly a member of Sir John A. Macdonald's cabinet. He was called to the bar of Nova Scotia in 1864, and was private secretary successively to Sir Dominick Daly, governor of Prince Edward Island, and Sir R. G. Macdonnell and Sir Hastings Doyle, governors of Nova Scotia. He was also Provincial A.D.C. to Sir William Fenwick Williams.

He was sworn into office July 14, 1890.

INDEX.

ACADIA, ancient limits of, 3
  College, 282, 286, 287
Acadian lands, resettlement of, 79
Acadians, expulsion of, 79
Academy at Windsor, 193, 196
Act for the establishment of religion, 39, 44
Adams, John, 21
Agnew, Rev. John, 15, 17, 18
Alexander, Sir William, 4
Alline, Rev. Henry, 277, 278
Almon, W. J., 246
Andrews, Rev. Samuel, 152, 155, 158
Annapolis county, Dr. Breynton visits, 86
Annapolis mission, account of, 90, 91
Anwell, Rev. William, 34
Archdeaconries established, 219
Archibald, Sir A. G. Governor, 310, 311
  Samuel G. W., 46
Argall, Capt. Samuel, 4
Arnold, Major General, 205
  Rev. Oliver, 155, 158, 159
Auchmuty, Rev. Samuel, 121
  James, 246
Avery, Rev. Richard, 126, 236

BADGER, Rev. Moses, 102, 104, 155, 159, 161
Bailey, Rev. Jacob, 36
Bailly, Mr., 192
Baptist churches founded, 278, 279

Barclay, Col. de Lancey, 206
  Rev. Henry, 36
  Thomas, 246
Beardsley, Rev. John, 149, 150, 156, 161, 162
Bedle, John, 247
Belcher, Andrew, 60
  Sir Edward, 60
  Jonathan, 60, 63
Bennett, Rev. Joseph, 72, 73
Bermuda, 219, 220
Berrian's History of Trinity Church, New York, 120
Berton, Peter, 248
Best, Rev. George, 219
Biard, Father Peter, 6, 10
Billopp, Christopher, 248
Binney, Edward, 239
  Bishop Hibbert, 238, 242
  Rev. Hibbert, 238
  Jonathan, 239, 249
Bissett, Rev. George, 151, 156, 162, 163
Bliss, Daniel, 249
  John Murray, 249
  Jonathan, 250
  Hon. Judge, 239
  Mary, 239
Blowers, Sampson Salter, 197, 250
Bonnell, Isaac, 251
Botsford, Amos, 146, 251
Breda, Treaty of, 5
Brenton, James, 251
Breynton, Rev. John, 58, 59, 86
Brinley, George, 252
Browne, Rev. Arthur, 35

Browne, Rev. Isaac, 104, 156, 163, 165
Brudenell, Rev. Mr., 156, 165
Bryzelius, Rev. Paulus, 74
Budd, Elisha, 252
Bulkeley, Richard, 197
Burger, Rev. Mr., 54
Byles, Rev. Mather, 102, 152, 156, 165, 167

CALVINISTS at Lunenburg, 69, 70
Campbell, Sir Colin, 304
　Lord William, Governor, 296
Campobello, 151
Caner, Rev. Henry, 35, 102, 156, 168
Canso, 23, 24
Carleton, Sir Guy, 99
Carroll, Rev. John, 45
Champlain, 8
Chandler, Joshua, 253
　Rev. Thomas Bradbury, 117, 131, 134
Chebucto Bay, 25
Cheever, Rev. Israel, 275
Chicken Cock Church in Halifax, 28
Chipman, Ward, 253
Church Diocesan Society, 234
　lands in Nova Scotia, 222, 223
Churches in Nova Scotia, how aided, 224
Churchmanship of Nova Scotia, 287, 288
Churchmen become Baptists, 65, 66, 279
Clarke, Rev. Richard Samuel, 152, 156, 158, 159
　Rev. William, 156, 170
Clergymen at Bishop Courtney's Consecration, 243, 244
　in Diocese before 1830, 225, 226

Cleveland, Rev. Aaron, 272, 273
Cochran, James, 236
　Sir James, 206
　Miss, 236
　Hon. Thomas, 236
　Judge Thomas, 236
　General William, 207, 236
　William, S. T. D., 197, 200
Cock, Rev. Daniel, 274
Cogswell, Hon. Hezekiah, 208, 233
Collins, Enos, 254
Comingo, Rev. Bruin Romcas, 274
Commissary in New Brunswick, 218
Congregational churches in Nova Scotia, 275, 276
Cooke, Rev. Samuel, 150, 151, 170–172, 218
Cornwallis, church built at, 82
　Governor, 26, 294
　mission at, 84
Cossitt, Rev. Ranna, 215, 216
Coster, Rev. George, 219
Courtney, Bishop Frederic, 240, 242–244
Crawley, Rev. Edmund A., 286
Creighton, John, 254
Croke, Judge Alexander, 201
Crooke, Margaret, 128
　John, 128
Cumberland County during the Revolution, 93, 94
　mission, account of, 91, 94
Cunard, Abraham, 255
　Robert, 255
　Sir Samuel, 255
Cunningham, Richard, 255
Cuthbert, Rev. Robert, 18, 19
Cutler, Rev. Timothy, 35

DALHOUSIE College, 282–286
　Earl of, 283, 284, 302
Daly, Malachy Bowes, Governor, 313

Index. 317

Davidson, Hugh, 26
De Guercheville, Marquise, 269
De la Loutre, Louis Joseph, 269
De Lancey, James, 256
De la Roche, Rev. Peter, 74, 107
De la Tour, Charles, 4, 5
  Claude, 4
De Monts, 3, 8
Des Brisay, Rev. Theophilus, 216
Des Enclaves, Mons., 269
De Seitz, Baron, 63
De Subercase, M., 11
Dibblee, Rev. Frederick, 152
Digby, 98, 107
Dissenters, first Protestant, 271
Dissenting church in Halifax, 272
Douglas, Sir Charles, 137
Doyle, Sir Charles Hastings, 308, 309
  Lawrence O'Connor, 45
Duke of Kent, 29, 300, 301

EAGLESON, Rev. J., 91-94, 216
Ellis, Governor, 296
  Rev. William, 82, 84, 85
Episcopate in America, plans for, 109-111
  in Nova Scotia, plan for, 114-116

FAIRBANKS, Hon. Charles Rufus, 46, 209
Falkland, Governor, 305
Falmouth, mission at, 84
Finucane, Chief Justice, 63
First Assembly of Nova Scotia, 38
Fisher, Rev. Nathaniel, 156, 172, 173
Fitz Clarence, Lady Amelia, 305
Francklin, James Boutineau, 197

Francklin, Hon. Michael, 197, 256
  Mrs. Susanna, 197
Fredericton, 151, 152
  Diocese of, 225
Friar Lawrence's Cell, 29

GANNETT, Rev. Caleb, 275
George, Sir Rupert Dennis, 236
Goreham, Capt. John, 26
Graham, Rev. Hugh, 274
Gray, Rev. Benjamin G., 143
Green, Benjamin, 26
  Francis, 257
Guysborough, 98

HAGUE, Rev. Dyson, 59
Halhead, Edward, 34, 35
Haliburton, Judge T. C., 46, 258
Halliburton, Sir Brenton, 63, 129, 259
Halifax, founding of, 27, 28
  chief buildings of, 30-32
  description of, 28-30
  Earl of, 27
  German settlers in, 27
  refounding of, 31-33
  population of, 57
Hamilton, John, 23
  Otho, 23
Handfield, John, 22, 23
Hants County, Dr. Breynton visits, 86
Harrison, Rev. John, 16, 17
Harvey, Sir John, Governor, 305
Hill, Rev. George W., 66
Hobley, Mr., 192
Hole, Rev. Charles, 59
Honyman, Rev. James, 21, 35
Hopson, Governor, 294
Horton, mission at, 84
Houseal, Rev. Bernard Michael, 156, 173, 215
Hulme, Lieut.-Col., 209
Howe, Capt. Edward 26

Howe, Hon. Joseph, Governor, 310, 390

INGLIS, Anne, 129
  Rev. Archibald Peane, 107, 196, 197
  Bishop Charles, 117-131, 156, 193, 194
  Dr. Charles, 236
  Bishop John, 218-221, 231-237
  General Sir J. E. W., 212, 214, 236
  Margaret, 128, 129
  Thomas, 236

JESUIT Missions in Acadia, 6, 269
Johnston, Judge James William, 259, 310
Rev. Samuel, 35
Jordan, Rev. Robert, 36

KEMPT, Governor, 302
King George II., death of, 61
King's College, Act for founding, 198
  buildings, charter, etc., 200
  early statutes, of, 202-205
  first governors of, 201
  pre-charter students at, 205-210
  students at, 210, 212
Kings County, Dr. Breynton visits, 86
Kniphausen, Baron, 63

LAND of Evangeline, 67, 68
Lawrence, Governor, 62, 295
Legge, Governor, 297
Le Marchant, Sir John G., Governor, 306
Lescarbot, Marc, 9
Lords of Trade, 33
Loyalist clergy in the Revolution, 100-105

Loyalists, attention of, directed to New Brunswick, 146
  come to St. John in 1783, 147
  emigration of, 96-98
  new settlements made by, 98, 106
  provision for, 99
  of the Revolution, 95, 96
  sufferings of, 100
Ludlow, George Duncan, 261
Lunenburg, 28
  reports from mission at, 76, 77
Lutheran Church at Lunenburg, 274
Lutherans at Lunenburg, 69, 70
Lyon, Rev. Mr., 276

MACDONNELL, Sir R. G., Governor, 307
Maillard, Antoine Simon, 270
Maitland, Governor, 303
Malcolm, Rev. Mr., 35
Malecites, 6
Mariotti, M., 237
Marriage by license and by banns, 48-52
  licenses, transfer of, 50
Marshall, Rev. John Rutgers, 156, 173, 174
Mascarene, Paul, 11, 26
Mather's Church in Halifax, 273
McConnell's History of the Church, 109
McLelan, Archibald W., Governor, 312
Medley, Bishop John, 153, 154
Micmacs, 6
Missionaries in 1807, 215
Missions in New Brunswick, account of, in 1799, 152
  state of, in 1799, 108
Montagu, Lord Charles Greville, 63
Moore, Rev. William, 273, 275

Index. 319

Morden, James, 261
Moreau, Rev. Jean Baptiste, 34, 70–72
Mulgrave, Earl, Governor, 306
Murdoch, Rev. James, 274

NEW BRUNSWICK, first officials of, 150
   first settlers in, 148
   settlement of, 145
   made a separate province in 1784, 147
   University of, 201
Newfoundland, missions in, 219, 220
New Light movement, 277, 278
Newport, mission at, 84
Nicholson, Governor Francis, 11, 15, 290
Norris, Rev. Robert, 152
Nova Scotia, the ancient Acadia, 4
   Baronets of, 4
   description of, 4

ODELL, Rev. Jonathan, 150, 156, 174–177
Old Missions in 1784, 105, 106

PANTON, Rev. George, 107, 139, 156, 177
Parr, Governor John, 63, 137, 297
Parishes formed at Shelburne, 139,
   joined, 142
Peden, Mr., 23, 24
Pepperell, Sir William, 141
Phelps, Rev. Benaiah, 275
Philipps, Governor, 291
Phips, Sir William, 5
Pidgeon, Rev. George, 152
Pigott, Rev. George, 20
Plant, Rev. Matthias, 35
Port Rossignol (Liverpool), 85
Port Royal, 4, 8
Presbyterian Church in Lunenburg, 273

Presbytery established, 274
Prevost, Governor, 301
Prince Edward Island, mission in, 216
Prince William Henry, 137, 300
Putnam, James, 261
Pryor, Rev. John, 286

RYSWICK, Treaty of, 5
Ruggles, General Timothy, 263
   Rev. John Owen, 263
Recollets in Acadia, 269
"Revival" under Henry Alline, 277, 278
Richey, Matthew Henry, Governor, 312
Robinson, Beverly, Jr., 135, 262
Rowland, Rev. John Hamilton, 107, 139, 142, 144, 156, 177, 178
   Rev. Thomas Bolby, 142, 143

SALISBURY, John, 26
Sayre, Rev. James, 156, 178
   Rev. John, 104, 146, 150, 156, 179, 180
School lands in Nova Scotia, 192
Scovil, Rev. James, 152, 156, 180, 181
Seabury, Bishop, 103, 114
Secombe, Rev. John, 275
Sewall, Jonathan, 264
Sharrock, Ralph, 192
Shelburne, founding and fate of, 135, 138
   in 1799, 144
   churches built at, 139, 141
   Earl of, 141
Sherbrook, Governor, 302
Shreve, Rev. Thomas, 107
Smith, Rev. David, 274
S. P. C. K., gifts of books, 223, 224

Spencer, Rev. A. G., 219
S. P. G., financial Aid to Diocese, 221
schools in Nova Scotia, 191, 193
Stanser, Bishop Robert, 59, 218, 227–231
Mrs. Robert, 63, 231
Stout, Hon. Richard, 238
Stuart, Gilbert, 265
St. Andrews, 151
St. Croix Island, 3
St. Germains, Treaty of, 4
St. John chartered in 1785, 147
St. Paul's Church, Charlottetown, 216
St. Paul's Church, Halifax, 53, 60
burials in, 63, 64
mural tablets, etc., in, 62
quarrel over rectorship, 64
rectors of, 59, 60
parish organized, 59, 60
Strange, Chief Justice, portrait by Benjamin West, 33
Sydney, Cape Breton, 216

THOMAS, Nathaniel Ray, 265
Toleration of Dissent, 39
Townsend, Rev. Epenetus, 156, 181
Trinity Church, St. John, 152
Tutty, Rev. William, 33, 35, 54
Twining, Rev. John Thomas, 281
Rev. William, 64, 65

UNIACKE, Judge Richard John, 46, 201, 209
Utrecht, Treaty of, 3

VETCH, Governor, 289, 291

Viets, Rev. Roger, 107, 156, 181, 182
Vincent, Rev. Robert, 73, 74
Vining, Miss, 128

WALTER, Rev. William, 107, 139, 143, 144, 156, 182–184
Wallis, Provo, 266
Sir Provo W. P., 266
Watts, Rev. Richard, 19, 20
Weeks, Rev. Joshua Wingate, 59, 90, 156, 184–186
Wentworth, Benning, 201
Sir John, 29, 32, 63, 201, 267, 298–301
Wesleyan body in Nova Scotia, 280, 281
Westfield, mission of, 152
Weymouth, 98
Whig legislation against Tories, 146
Whigs enter Trinity Church, 122
White, Bishop, Letter of Bishop Inglis to, 217
Capt. Gideon, 135
Rev. Thomas Howland, 143
Wilkins, Rev. Isaac, 156, 186–189
Williams, Sir Fenwick, Governor, 307, 308
Willis, Rev. Robert, 64, 65
Wilmot, and mission at, 84, 98
Governor, 296
Windsor, chapel built at, 82
suitable place for school, 194
Wiswell, Rev. John, 90, 107, 156, 189
Wood, Rev. Thomas, 35, 57, 61, 62, 72, 85, 89, 270, 275
Woodstock, mission at, 152

www.ingramcontent.com/pod-product-compliance
Lightning Source LLC
Chambersburg PA
CBHW021158230426
43667CB00006B/448